# ELECTRONIC RECORDING
## of
# INTERROGATIONS

Library of Congress Control Number: 2005926315

ISBN 0-9760093-3-1

Published by John E. Reid & Associates, Inc.
250 S. Wacker Dr. Suite 1200, Chicago, IL 60606
www.Reid.com
Designed and printed by Hahn Printing Incorporated
752 North Adams Road, Eagle River, Wisconsin  54521

First Edition, First Printing

# Table of Contents

# Preface

John E. Reid and Associates is a private corporation established in 1947 in Chicago, Illinois. The company offers detection of deception services to clients in law enforcement, private industry and the legal community. Over the years our firm has conducted field research and published studies in the area of interviewing and behavior symptom analysis. We have also developed and refined interrogation techniques that were found to be successful in learning the truth from guilty suspects. These efforts culminated in a structured approach to interviewing and interrogation known as "The Reid Technique of Interviewing and Interrogation®." This well-defined and very successful technique of conducting an interview and interrogation has been described in text books and presented in a variety of training programs. Each year thousands of investigators from private, government and law enforcement sectors attend three and four-day seminars presented by John E. Reid and Associates to learn The Reid Technique of Interviewing and Interrogation. These seminars are taught in the United States, Canada, Mexico, Europe and Asia.

Over the last fifty years, John E. Reid and Associates has established an international reputation of expertise in the fields of interviewing and interrogation. This reputation is respected not only by investigators but also criminal courts. The United States Supreme Court, as well as state and federal courts, have favorably referenced our text book and training manual in deciding cases involving confession admissibility. Members of our staff are consulted to offer expert testimony in the area of proper and improper interviewing and interrogation techniques in criminal and civil trials.

Over the past several years it has been established on a number of occasions that innocent people have falsely confessed to a crime that they did not commit. As a result, police interrogation techniques have come under closer scrutiny by both the courts and various state legislative bodies. One of the remedies that both institutions have embraced is the requirement to electronically record police interviews and interrogations. In fact, a number of police agencies have instituted policies that all of their interrogations are to be electronically recorded even though their state legislature or courts have not yet mandated such a requirement.

This book, *Electronic Recording of Interrogations*, is designed to offer police interrogators some insight into the issues to consider and the guidelines to follow when preparing to conduct an interview or interrogation that will be electronically recorded. As this practice develops over the next several years more will be learned about how judges, juries, prosecutors and defense attorneys view police interrogation techniques. However based on the experience of Alaska and Minnesota police officers who have electronically recorded their interrogations for 20 and 11 years respectively, if conducted properly, the overwhelming majority of electronically recorded confessions will be found admissible by the courts.

This book was written for a number of different audiences: (1) for those investigators and departments who are under a legal mandate to electronically record interviews and interrogations; (2) for those investigators and agencies who have or are considering enacting an in-house policy concerning electronic recording; and, (3) for prosecutors and judges to help juries understand the interrogation process and to shape laws that permit effective interrogation techniques while at the same time protecting the innocent and guarding against false confessions.

The authors would like to thank Joseph P. Buckley, President of John E. Reid & Associates, Inc for his assistance in the development of this book and Broward County Sheriff's Department for sharing their experiences electronically recording interviews and interrogations.

Due to the special nature of this book, with its discourse between interrogator and suspect, the words *he* and *him* are used generically in order to avoid redundancy. Also the use of the words *suspect* and *subject* are generic terms used interchangeably throughout the book and refer to a person who is being interviewed.

# Chapter 1

## INTRODUCTION

### Historical Overview of Electronic Recording of Interviews and Interrogations

There has always been an aura of secrecy and intrigue surrounding police interviews and interrogations. Over the years criminal investigators have developed specific techniques in an effort to learn the truth from suspects. Examples include the "good cop-bad cop" approach, "playing one suspect against the other," lying to suspects about having incriminating evidence linking the person to the crime, minimizing the moral seriousness of the suspect's crime, expressing sympathy toward the suspect's decision to commit the crime and suggesting reasons and excuses that led up to the suspect's decision to commit the crime. Many of these interrogation techniques rely extensively on pretense and duplicity. It is, therefore, understandable that investigators were reluctant to publicly disclose these techniques to criminals who may benefit greatly from this knowledge and, thus, fortify their resistance to telling the truth.

As effective interrogation techniques were being developed, so too were devices to electronically record sounds and images. As audiovisual recording technology became more affordable and compact, there were suggestions that, in an effort to evaluate the legality and voluntariness of a confession, it would be advantageous for police to electronically record interrogations. The law enforcement community initially did not react favorably to this suggestion.

Certainly there was a concern that a visual or audiotaped interrogation would reveal secrets to the criminal world and consequently decrease the effectiveness of interrogation tactics. Of greater concern, however, was that electronic recordings violated the suspect's privacy. From years of experience, investigators recognized that suspects are much more likely to tell the truth in a private environment. An unspoken concern, however, may have been that many interrogation practices, deemed necessary to elicit information, would not hold up to legal scrutiny when viewed in a court of law.

In the 1970's and 80's an effective way for a defense attorney to attack a confession was to argue that the defendant's waiver of Miranda rights was inadequate.[1]  Initially enacted as a means to establish compliance with the Miranda decision, the states of Alaska and Minnesota required that all custodial interviews and interrogations be electronically recorded.

In the 1990's DNA evidence achieved acceptance within the legal community which resulted in a number of overturned convictions. These cases revealed, not only that innocent defendants had been wrongfully convicted, but also that some of those defendants had offered false confessions following police interrogations. These findings caused greater concern about what was going on behind the closed door of the

---

[1] The 1966 <u>Miranda</u> decision required that prior to questioning a suspect who was in custody, the police must first advise the suspect of his right to remain silent and right to an attorney and also seek a waiver of those constitutional rights.

interrogation room.

During this same time, there was a growing academic interest in false confessions which produced a number of laboratory studies and published research. While this research did not prove that standard police interrogation techniques induced an innocent suspects to confess, it did suggest possible mechanisms whereby a false confession could be elicited.[2] In an effort to develop empirical evidence to support laboratory theory, a number of researchers collected anecdotal cases in which it was claimed that an innocent person was either wrongfully charged or convicted of a crime, or coerced into confessing.[3]

The apparent epidemic of detected and undetected false confessions occurring across the United States generated a media frenzy calling for police interrogation reform. Courts and the public were demanding police to electronically record interrogations.[4] Many departments and agencies voluntarily established internal guidelines for electronic recording of interviews and interrogations.[5] After DNA evidence exonerated a number of inmates on death row the state of Illinois, in 2005, became the third state to require electronic recording of some interviews and interrogations. Just as the 1966 Miranda decision was

---

[2] Kassen, S. and McNawl, K. "Police Interrogation and Confessions: Communicating Promises and Threats by Pragmatic Implication." Law and Human Behavior, 1991, 12: 233-251.

[3] Bedau, H. & Radelet, M., "Miscarriages of Justice in Potential Capital Cases," *Stanford Law Review,* 40, 21-179, 1987; Ofshe, R. & Leo, R., "The Consequences of False Confessions: Deprivation of Liberty and Miscarriages of Justice in the Age of Psychological Interrogation."*Journal of Criminal Law and Criminology,* 88, 1998.

[4] Report of the Illinois Governor's Commission on Capital Punishment (April 2002).

[5] Sullivan, T. "Police Experiences with Recording Custodial Interrogations" <u>Northwest University School of Law Center on Wrongful Convictions</u>. No. 1 Summer, 2004.

designed to assure that every suspect's constitutional rights were upheld, requiring electronic recording of interrogations has been perceived as a panacea to remedy false confessions. The expectation of having an interrogation electronically recorded has grown to the extent that if no recording is made police misconduct is implied. A Massachusetts Supreme Court recently ruled that if an interrogation is not electronically recorded, the judge's instructions to the jury must include a statement that the defendant's confession be viewed with caution.[6] Alaska was the first state to require law enforcement to electronically record interrogations in 1985, Minnesota followed in 1994 and Illinois in 2005.[7]

Also in 2005, the state of New Jersey required that for a confession to be admissible as evidence it must be electronically recorded.[8] There have been 21 other states that have considered proposals to require electronic recording of interrogations since 2001, the most recent being; New York, Maryland, Connecticut, Oregon, and Missouri. The District of Columbia statute 17 requires the Chief of Police to adopt a general order that would require police to electronically record interrogations of persons suspected of dangerous crimes or crimes of violence. Even though not required by law to electronically record conversations with suspects, there are 238 law enforcement agencies that voluntarily electronically record custodial interrogations.[9] Surveys of law enforcement agencies nationally have found that videotaping was used to some extent by one third of all police departments in jurisdictions with populations over 50,000.[10]

---

[6] *Commonwealth v. DiGiambattista,* 813 N.E.2d 516 (2004).

[7] Stephan v. State, 711 P.2d 1156, 1158 Alaska 1985; State v. Scales, 518 N.W. 2d 587 Minnesota, 1994; Public Act 93-0206, HB 223, Illinois 2005.

[8] New Jersey Lawyer Vol 14, No. 2 1/10/05.

[9] Sullivan, T. "Police Experiences with Recording Custodial Interrogations" <u>Northwest University School of Law Center on Wrongful Convictions.</u> No. 1 Summer, 2004.

Electronic Recording of custodial interrogations is not unique to the United States; several other countries have also adopted the practice. In the early 1990's the Police Executive Committee of New Zealand approved the videotaping of police interview and interrogations on a national basis, Great Britain has required electronic recording since 1984 (Police and Criminal Evidence Act of 1984), Canada and Australia police are required to electronically record interrogations where practical, Tasmania has required videotaping of interviews since 2001, and the Hong Kong Immigration Department and Customs and Excise Department have been introducing tape-recording and video-recording of interviews as equipment becomes available.

Whether electronic recording will actually decrease the number of false confessions obtained during a police interrogation has yet to be determined. What can be said with certainty is that an increasing number of states will eventually require electronic recording. In the not too distant future, electronic recording of interviews and interrogations will be as accepted a practice by law enforcement as the investigator's use of computer technology is today.

---

[10] U.S. Department of Justice, Office of Justice Programs, National Institute of Justice, Geller, Videotaping Interrogations and Confessions, DOJ HV 7635. U548 G318 (1993).

# Research and Surveys Relating to Electronic Recording

In the early 1980's the Tasmanian Police Department conducted a trial experiment with recording suspect interrogations. This early experience with electronic recording was not considered very successful as the following conclusion reveals:

> *"Significantly, since the tape-recording experiment commenced, the number of persons interviewed at the station has decreased; the number of persons making confessions during interrogation has decreased, and the number charged has decreased. As a result, the crime clean-up rate has also decreased. Increases have been shown of the following: 1) refusal of suspects to speak at all, 2) refusal to admit other offenses, and 3) refusal to nominate co-offenders."* [11]

While these findings are hardly scientific, they do support the common-sense notion that a suspect who is aware that his statements are being memorialized on magnetic tape will be reluctant to incriminate himself or others. Another implied finding is that possibly investigators are less effective in conducting interrogations when they know the session is being electronically recorded.

By the 1990's there was a growing interest in electronic recording of interrogations in the United States. The National Institute of Justice (NIJ) funded a national survey to investigate the frequency in which law enforcement agencies utilized videotaping technology related to questioning

---

[11] Scientific and Technical Aids to Police Interview-Interrogation Det.Sgt Luppo Prins, Tasmanian Police.1982-83 Reported in Inbau, Reid & Buckley, Criminal Interrogation and Confessions, 3rd ed. Williams and Wilkins, 177-178, 1986.

of suspects and their experiences with the practice.[12]  Out of 2,400 law enforcement agencies surveyed 384 (16%) videotaped interviews, interrogations or confessions.  Undoubtedly this figure would have been higher if audio-recorded sessions were also included. The questionnaire completed by the agencies did not specify what part of the interaction between the suspect and investigator was videotaped.  From our experience the most common practice from that era would be for only the confession to be videotaped.

The NIJ report indicated that most responding departments expressed positive experiences with videotaping.  Specifically, the videotape (1) was helpful in court to establish the trustworthiness and voluntariness of the confession, (2) was beneficial to help an investigator prepare for testimony and, (3) defend against allegations of improper interrogation tactics.  Of the 2,016 departments who chose not to videotape any part of the questioning process, two primary reasons were offered for this decision.  The first was a concern that a videotape would increase defense claims of improper interrogation tactics.  Second, was a fear that videotaping the interrogation would inhibit a suspect's willingness to tell the truth.

While this report echoed the previous perception that electronic recording decreases a suspect's willingness to tell the truth, it did not offer any specific support for that finding.  It did, however, cite three important aspects of electronic recording that were found to be beneficial to law enforcement.  For the first time, electronic recording was viewed as a possible aid to law enforcement.

---

[12] Geller, W.A., "Videotaping Interrogations and Confessions" *National Institute of Justice Research in Brief,* Washington, D.C. March, 1993.

In the meantime interviewing and interrogation techniques continued to evolve and court decisions further clarified legal issues surrounding interrogations and confessions. By1994 two states, Minnesota and Alaska, both had Supreme Court decisions that required electronic recording of all custodial interrogations.   During this period law enforcement agencies recognized that interviewing and interrogation had become a very specialized skill that required specific training.  It was the combination of both these events – required electronic recording and a group of investigators who received training in the same interrogation technique – that generated the unique opportunity to conduct the subsequent research project.

Eight hundred investigators from the states of Alaska and Minnesota who received training in the Reid Technique of Interviewing and Interrogation were asked to participate in a study concerning their personal experiences with required electronic recording within their state.[13] One hundred-twelve agreed to complete a questionnaire covering their last two years experience with required electronic recording.  During that time period these investigators conducted an estimated 9,375 interviews and 5,651 interrogations.

The reported experience with electronic recording by these investigators was, by and large, very favorable.  A small percentage of investigators, around 10%, reported negative experiences with electronic recording of interviews and interrogations.  This small group of investigators believed that the procedure most benefited the defense, increased the length of trials and felt the law had decreased their ability to

---

[13] Jayne, B. "Empirical Experiences of Required Electronic Recording of Interviews and Interrogations on Investigators' Practices and Case Outcomes" Law Enforcement Executive Forum, 4 (1) 103–112, 2004.  This study is reproduced in appendix A

perform duties. However, The vast majority of these investigators reported positive experiences with electronic recording, for example:

- 54% believed that electronic recording most benefited the prosecution
- 68% reported that electronic recording decreased the length of trials
- 47% supported the law and believed it should be passed in other states

This study shed more light on the recurring concern that electronic recording inhibits truth-telling. While 22% of the investigators believed that electronic recording decreased their confession rate, 74% believed that it did not affect their ability to elicit a confession. This finding was explored further by asking a question about the visibility of the recording device during an interview or interrogation, ranging from never being visible to always being visible. From each investigator's statistics, a confession rate was calculated. These finding are listed in table 1.

Table 1

Effect of Visibility of Recording Device on Confession Rates

| Condition | Confession Rate |
|-----------|-----------------|
| Never Visible | 82% |
| Sometimes Visible | 52% |
| Usually Visible | 50% |
| Always Visible | 43% |

This data clearly demonstrates that the more visible a recording device the lower the investigator's confession rate. The finding strongly suggests that a camera or tape recorder should be concealed or positioned in a non-obtrusive area of the room in an effort to minimize the visual reminder that the interview or interrogation is being electronically recorded.

The Jayne study focused on individual investigators' experiences and perceptions with electronic recording in two states that required electronic recording by law. However, many agencies electronically record interviews and interrogations on their own volition. In an effort to generate support for requiring electronic recording of all police interrogations, Sullivan contacted 238 law enforcement agencies in 31 states who were known to record custodial interviews of suspects in felony investigations.[14] Appendix B lists these agencies, as well as information about their recording practices. The information gleaned from these departments yielded the following reported experiences:

- Most departments have no written regulations or guidelines that govern when and how recordings are to be conducted.

- Most agencies leave the recording decision to the discretion of the officer in charge.

- Most agencies begin the recording with the administration of Miranda rights and continue to record until the completion of the confession.

- Agencies are selective in determining what interviews will be recorded. Typically, only the interviews of suspects

---

[14] Sullivan, T. "Police Experiences with Recording Custodial Interrogations" Northwest University School of Law Center on Wrongful Convictions. No. 1 Summer, 2004

being questioned about a "serious" crime are recorded. Examples of these crimes include homicide, sexual assault, armed robbery, crimes against a person or crimes involving a weapon.

- There is no standard or customary approach to how an interview or interrogation is electronically recorded. There is a mixture of audio and audiovisual recordings. In the later instance, a variety of camera angles are represented, including the use of single or multiple cameras.

- "Virtually every officer… was enthusiastically in favor of the practice." [15]

As this literature review indicates, the entire concept of electronically recording police interviews and interrogations is so new that there is very little field research conducted on the phenomenon. The studies that have been published are primarily at the descriptive stage, where efforts have been made to establish how many departments are electronically recording interrogations, under what circumstances is the practice being employed, and how it is being done.

The truly fascinating aspects of electronically recording a police interrogation have barely been broached. A consistent statistical and empirical finding is that a suspect's knowledge of being electronically recorded does seem to inhibit the truth-telling process. However, there are exceptions. Some suspects appear more anxious to confess if they know that their statement will be permanently recorded and played in a public

---

[15] It must be remembered that the Sullivan report was conducted for the specific purpose of publishing results that could be cited in an effort to persuade courts or agencies to adopt a policy of electronically recording police interrogations.

forum. It would be of great benefit to the police to know if a particular suspect fit this profile.

There are bound to be evidential effects of an electronically recorded confession. Already there is laboratory research that demonstrates that the camera angle in simulated interrogations influences mock crime verdicts.[16] Will a study someday demonstrate that electronically recorded confessions increase conviction rates and reduce appeals? Or will electronic recordings produce a group of highly specialized defense experts who will attack police interrogation tactics by breaking the recorded statements down, word, for word, image by image resulting in monumental changes in police interrogation tactics? Will the age of electronic recordings mark the last chapter in police interrogations causing a substantial shift in our court system away from the current standard in which the spoken word represents the most common form of evidence presented in a court of law to an era where prosecutors rely primarily on forensic evidence to prove a case? No one knows the answers to these questions. But, these possibilities, good or bad, should be considered in any decision regarding electronic recording of interviews or interrogations.

# Pros and Cons of Electronic Recording

The surveys we reviewed expressed a number of consistently positive experiences with electronic recording of interviews and

---

[16] Lassiter, D. Et al., Criminal Confessions on Videotape: Does Camera Perspective Bias Their Perceived Veracity?, Current Research in Social Psychology, Vol. 7 No.1, 200

interrogations. But there were also reported problems. The following are some of the listed benefits and difficulties departments have experienced with electronic recording.

## Benefits of Electronic Recording

Proponents of required electronic recording of police interrogations primarily focus on the benefits in the courtroom such as resolving Miranda issues or establishing the voluntariness of a confession. As the following points indicate, electronic recording can also be beneficial during the course of the investigation to:

- *Assist in evaluating the suspect's behavior symptoms*
- *Document the suspect's denials and inconsistencies in their statements*
- *Document behaviors to refute other allegations*
- *Improve the accuracy and completeness of written reports*
- *Increase the personal safety of investigators*
- *Help investigators to develop their interviewing and interrogation skills*
- *Can be used by investigators as part of an interrogation technique*
- *Decrease the length of trials*
- *Document Miranda rights and waiver*
- *Document the suspect's appearance at the time of the interrogation*
- *Refresh the investigator's memory and help him prepare for trial*
- *Document the voluntariness of a confession*

## Perceived Disadvantages and Investigator Fears Regarding Electronic Recording

Our review of surveys and interviews with investigators and prosecutors who had experience with electronic recording of interviews and interrogations, indicated that there are documented instances where electronic recordings have produced negative experiences, but most were very pleased with the overall results. It was the investigators without electronically recording experience that expressed a variety of concerns about the prospect of electronically recording their interrogations. For example:

- *Loss of privacy – suspects will not confess if electronically recorded*
- *Cost to agency makes electronic recording an unreasonable burden to the department*
- *There are too many potential technical problems that may result in confessions being suppressed*
- *Unrecorded voluntary confessions may be suppressed*
- *Departments do not have room to store all of the recordings*
- *Electronic recordings will give the defense information that a defense expert can use against the prosecution*
- *Electronic recording will be used by the defense to identify inconsistencies in statements*
- *Electronic recordings will allow defense attorneys to attack interrogation tactics*
- *Investigator statements will be taken out of context*

- *Judges and juries may not understand police interrogation tactics*

These concerns and others expressed by prosecutors and investigators will be addressed in subsequent chapters of this book.

# Conclusion

This Chapter has offered an overview of electronically recording police interrogations and suspect's confessions. While only a few states currently require electronic recording of interrogations under certain circumstances, many individual departments and agencies have developed their own policies governing electronic recording of interviews and interrogations.

The remaining chapters of this book will address the issues introduced in the present chapter. Chapter 2 will describe the physical aspects of setting up an interview room for electronic recording. Chapter 3 addresses the investigator's conduct during an interview or interrogation that is electronically recorded. Chapter 4 offers recommendations for electronic recording under special circumstances such as the interview of a victim in a child sexual assault, multiple investigator interrogations and multiple suspect interrogations. Chapter 5 presents an overview of the Reid Technique of Interviewing and Interrogation and offers suggestions to assist investigators when testifying.

Apart from legal decisions and published articles, the information presented in the subsequent chapters was derived from numerous sources. The Broward County Sheriff's Department was very helpful in providing their proposals for electronic recording as well as their in-house policy manual.    A technical expert with many years of experience installing camera and microphones in police interview rooms was instrumental in writing Chapter 2.    Prosecutors from the states of Minnesota, Alaska and Illinois were interviewed and provided insight from that side of the bench. Dozens of investigators across the United States have also shared their personal experiences with electronic recording with the authors during training seminars.    Finally, Joe Buckley, president of John E. Reid & Associates, Inc, has participated in committees during the development of the Illinois law regulating electronic recording.

# Chapter 2

## PHYSICAL ASPECTS OF RECORDING[17]

There are a number of decisions to make with respect to the equipment and facilities necessary to electronically record an interview and interrogation. For example, the type of microphone or camera to use, the placement of the recording equipment, the best medium to initially save the recordings and how to preserve them for court use. In making these decisions it is important to keep in mind that the ultimate purpose for electronically recording is to memorialize the interview, interrogation and confession so that it can be used as evidence in a court of law.

There are a number of benefits that can be realized by electronically recording interrogations and confessions, including the ability to document that the Miranda warnings were properly given to the suspect and that a knowing and intelligent waiver was made; the ability to refute allegations that improper interrogation tactics were used; and the ability to document exactly what the suspect said during his confession. However, when something goes wrong with the recording process or the retrieval of the recording, these benefits can quickly become a liability for the prosecution. For example, in one case an audiotaped interrogation had seven minutes of

---

[17] The authors wish to thank Bruce Montgomery for sharing his expertise in helping write this chapter. Bruce is the President of Disclosure Video Systems located in Gurnee, IL. He has been in law enforcement for over 18 years and has 13 years of experience in electronic surveillance service and design.

distorted and garbled sound. The defense was successful in arguing that an improper promise of leniency was made during that portion of the interrogation. In another case the defense attorney alleged that improper interrogation procedures were utilized during the questioning of his client when he was able to establish that the police department had equipment available to electronically record the interrogation but chose not to do so in the present case.

When any of the following circumstances occur they will give the defense an opportunity to suggest that something was improperly done during the interrogation that the investigating officers do not want the court to know:

1.    The recording is misplaced and unavailable for trial.

2.    The recording equipment malfunctioned or the recording medium was corrupt, the result of which was that no recording was made.

3.    Portions of the recording are missing because of a mechanical failure.

4.    Portions of the audio recording are unintelligible (too soft, indistinct)

5.    The suspect cannot be seen on the video because the investigator stepped in front of the camera.

Whether a law enforcement agency decides to enact its own internal policy concerning electronic recording of interviews and interrogations or is required to do so by a court decision or statute, a clear lesson presents itself – the decision to electronically record interviews and interrogations should not be a half-hearted one. If electronic recordings are going to be made, the agency should be willing to spend the time and money to make sure that they are done right.

# Preliminary Decisions

Once the decision has been made to electronically record interviews and interrogations, the first consideration is whether the recordings should be audio or audiovisual. Audio recordings are, without question, less expensive to make and more convenient to obtain because of the compact size of tape recorders. Most legal decisions and state statutes leave both recording options open to the investigator. However, while not required by law, the preferred recording medium appears to be audiovisual in a fixed location, i.e., in the interview room. The reason for this goes back to the rationale for recording interviews and interrogations in the first place – as a means of enhancing the credibility of evidence against the defendant.

While an audiotape can document what was or was not said during an interrogation session with the police, it can also leave a great deal to the imagination. At the time a particular statement was made was the investigator standing over the suspect pointing a .357 Magnum at his head? Was the investigator gesturing with a closed fist when a question was asked? Did the investigator position his chair between the suspect and the door and aggressively move to within inches of the suspect's face when eliciting the first admission of guilt? In all probability none of these things occurred but the audiotape makes it difficult to refute the possibility that they did. The inability to see the interrogator or the suspect gives the defense an opportunity to cast an element of doubt as to whether the defendant's confession was, in fact, obtained in a legally acceptable manner.

Regardless of whether an agency decides to utilize an audio or audiovisual taped medium, a second important question to answer is whether the recording equipment should be in plain view of the suspect (overt), or hidden from the suspect's view (covert). There is no question that having recording equipment in full view inhibits some suspects from telling the truth. It is our recommendation, therefore, that recording equipment be positioned in such a way that the suspect is not constantly reminded that his statements are being recorded. The negative impact that electronic recording can have on a person's decision to tell the truth is always an important consideration, as the following experience illustrates:

A bank discovered a mysterious disappearance of $2,000 and a number of employees were scheduled for interviews in our office as part of an internal investigation. Eventually a 19-year-old female employee was interviewed. Prior to the interview the suspect was given a written release form requesting permission to tape-record her conversations while in the room, which she signed. Based on deceptive behavior observed during the interview, the employee was confronted with the fact that the investigator believed that she stole the missing money. After 35 minutes of interrogation the employee put her head down and stated that she would talk to the investigator about the missing money, but not in that room. Even though more than an hour had elapsed since signing the permission form allowing electronic recording, and even though the recording equipment was hidden behind a one-way mirror, the suspect was still very aware that a recording was being made and would not confess on camera. Only after being escorted to a room that was not wired for recording did the suspect offer a full confession.

# Recording Equipment

*Audio recording*

Over the years the authors have reviewed many electronically recorded interviews and interrogations conducted across the United States. Regardless of whether the recording was audiovisual or just audio, the most common problem we have encountered is a poor audio recording where portions of the conversation are garbled, too soft, mumbled, or indistinct and therefore, impossible to understand. The majority of the benefits that electronically recorded interviews and interrogations provide hinge on the ability to clearly hear and understand everything that what was said during the session. The judge and jury need to know whether Miranda warnings were properly administered, whether there was a valid waiver of those rights, whether the suspect was offered a promise of leniency or threatened in any way, and whether the suspect really did confess. It may be impossible to answer these questions if there is a problem with the audio recording. Consequently, a high quality audio recording should be a primary objective of any system.

To obtain a clear audio recording requires that background sounds be eliminated or reduced.  For this reason, as well as psychological ones, interview and interrogation rooms should be located away from holding cells which tend to be quite noisy.  To further decrease outside noise, the walls of the interview room can be insulated and a solid hard-core door installed.  Unless the interview room is exclusively used for custodial interviews, the door should not have a lock on it.

If possible, the walls of the interview room should be insulated to decrease outside noise and internal echoes. If it is not practical to install insulation or acoustic-board on the walls, putting in a drop-ceiling and carpeting the floor can significantly improve the sound quality within the room.

The microphone used should be a high quality line-powered microphone. The Crown PZM11LL is a pressure zone microphone designed

for conference rooms, surveillance and security applications which satisfies these requirements. The microphone should be positioned out of sight, but near the suspect. In our interview rooms the microphone is fastened to the underside of the desk which is off to the suspect's side, approximately 2½ - 3 feet from the suspect's mouth. Covert microphones can be placed anywhere in the room as a disguised light switch.

The placement of The Crown PZM11LL microphone on the wall at the end of the table in the photo below is equidistant between the interviewer and subject ensuring clear audio recording of both parties.    The corner mounted camera is at the subject focus angle however the table obstructs the full view of the subject and the visible corner mount of the camera may distract the suspect.

Interrogation room with corner mounted
camera and light switch microphone

One of the most popular and inexpensive *Gain Micro Audio System* microphone is touted as being the smallest   and best in the world.  The preamp features low noise, high gain, and auto level adjustment.  The mike is very small for easy concealment and has a six-foot mike lead and plug-and-play cable terminations with RCA connectors.

Super High Gain Micro Audio System

One consultant recommended that the covert microphone be placed on the ceiling, approximately in the middle of the room. The reason for the high location is to prevent a suspect from sabotaging the microphone with gum or a pencil. The Black box along the window in Photo 2-A on the left houses the subject-focused camera.

Photo 2-A

Ceiling mounted microphone

**Ceiling mounted microphone**

The cone on the left is a sprinkler the microphone is the white square on the right.

If an audiocassette recorder is being used to make a stand-alone audio recording, the recorder should be located out of the suspect's sight. One possible arrangement is to place the tape recorder on the desk but behind the suspect's immediate line of sight. With respect to selection of audiotapes, only virgin (brand new) audiotapes should be used and 90-minute tapes are preferable to 120-minute tapes which tend to be weak and break easily. If possible, the tape should be leaderless, so when the recorder is on it will be recording.

## *Visual recording*

The camera can be positioned in a covert or overt manner. A covert camera is often disguised as some feature within the room, for example, a thermostat or smoke detector. The obvious advantage to covert video recording is that it does not inhibit the suspect from telling the truth. However, there are two disadvantages of using a covert camera. The first

Photo 2-B

is that the video quality is not as good as with an overt camera which can use a larger lens. Second, during an interview or interrogation the investigator may oftentimes sit directly in front of the suspect, and since many covert cameras often are placed in the wall across from the suspect at about eye level, the interrogator would be blocking a full view of the suspect. Therefore, the covert camera should not be positioned directly in front of the subject, but rather off to one side to make certain that the suspect is visible at all times as seen in Photo 2-B where the camera angle is off to the side positioned behind an observation mirror. While an overt camera provides a better video image having the camera openly visible can have an undesirable effect in that it violates the sense of privacy that the interrogator tries to establish. Perhaps the best compromise is to have a camera with a large lens installed in an observation room behind a two- way mirror. This arrangement affords a high-quality picture as well as privacy. In the absence of an observation room, it is desirable to place the overt camera in a location that does not constantly remind the suspect that he is being recorded.  For example, placing an overt camera in a ceiling corner where the camera is directed downward toward the suspect is preferable to placing the camera on a tripod located eight feet directly in front of the suspect. The camera location in the corner can show a full frontal view of the suspect and is far enough above eye level so as to not serve as a constant reminder that the session is being electronically recorded.

A number of manufacturers build corner-mounted overt cameras including Extreme CCTV, Silent Witness, Videolarm and GBC.  When deciding on which covert camera to use, one consideration is the camera's durability.  As one consultant explained, if a fragile camera is used and the suspect punches it, a damaged camera precludes the investigator from conducting the interview in that room. A corner-mounted camera should not have any protruding parts and should be placed high enough so that it cannot be grabbed by the suspect.  Most of these cameras are encased in a hard shell and can withstand a severe blow without compromising the video quality.

The one drawback to corner-mounted overt cameras is that they have a limited lens selection from 3 - 12mm.  This generally is not a concern provided that the interview room is not too large. By placing the suspect's chair toward the center of the room or on the center of the opposite wall, the focal length for the lens tends to work best. An arrangement to be avoided is having the suspect sit very close to the camera. A fish-eye lens is not recommended since it distorts the field of vision.

*Covert Snake CCD Color Video Cameras*

There are a number of snake cameras on the market that can be easily concealed and still provide a quality picture and an angle that will encompass most of the interview room.

The problem with pinhole lens cameras in the past has been the

poor quality picture and the narrow angle of the lens. Today's *snake cameras* with a pinhole lens delivers 380 lines of resolution and stealthy low light rating of 0.2 lux, which is excellent for color cameras. Some of the cameras use the latest generation interline transfer $\frac{1}{4}$"

CCD with 510 x 492 pixels. 1/50 to 1/120,000 electronic shutter gives you great performance in nearly all lighting conditions. If the 60° lens is mounted in the corner of a 8 x10' interview room it will show about 80% of the room. There are a few options available with different camera heads as illustrated in the pictures. Some of the camera heads appear to be the head of a screw others have a cone shaped head. The camera head is a miniscule .45" x .45" x .75" and the processor board, located 10" down the cable is only .275" thick x 1.15" square.

## Room Arrangement

The average department does not have the luxury of designing an ideal interview room starting at the blueprint stage. Rather, most departments will attempt to modify their present interview/interrogation rooms in such a way as to incorporate electronic recording. Because each existing interview room is unique, with its own individual strengths and weaknesses, a department may have to compromise and tolerate some less-than-ideal arrangements in exchange for other desired benefits.

A room designed for conducting interviews and interrogations should be small enough to afford a sense of privacy without causing claustrophobia, but it should not be so large as to allow the suspect to psychologically escape into open space. An approximate dimension of 8' x 10' satisfies both of these objectives. The color of the walls can affect a video recording. White semi-glossy walls or bright white walls distort the contrast viewing of the picture, causing the lighter tones to be overexposed. To achieve a good video contrast the walls of the interview room should be colored. One expert reported the best success with neutral tans or lighter blues.

The room should be furnished with two or three chairs and a table or desk. The chairs should all be similar in design, perhaps with slight padding on the seat and back and have no arms. Furthermore, the chairs should not be equipped with wheels or rollers nor should they be bolted to the floor. The investigator's chair should be positioned in the room so that it does not block the camera view. Obviously, if the suspect initially sits in the investigator's chair, he should be asked to move to the other chair.

Most recording systems (VHS, DVR (digital video recorder)) have internal clocks to document the current time and date. If this is not an option, a clock can be placed in the interview room on the wall behind the suspect. The face of the clock should be large enough to clearly read from the videotape.

The arrangement of furniture within an interview room is critical from both a psychological and legal perspective. In a non-custodial setting, the investigator's chair should not block the suspect's access to the door. If

Photo 2-C

the investigator does sit between the suspect and the door it could be viewed by the court as sending the message that "you are not free to leave." The desk or table should be positioned off to the side of the two chairs, to be used as a writing surface. It should not be positioned between the suspect and investigator as seen in Photo 2-C. A deceptive suspect would much prefer to have a barrier, such as a desk or table, between himself and the investigator because the separation will help to reduce the anxiety and fear he experiences when lying. This room arrangement is not conducive to detecting deception or encouraging truthfulness.

*Camera angle*

The primary legal purpose for videotaping an interview or interrogation (as opposed to an audiotape) is to refute claims of coercion, where an allegation is made that physical force was used to extract a confession. The second purpose, in non-custodial cases, is to demonstrate that the investigator did not block the suspect's exit from the room. All other legal aspects of the interrogation (Miranda rights and waiver, promises of leniency, confession, etc.) can be resolved through the audio recording.

Consequently, the camera need not show the entire interview room.[18] We believe that the best camera angle is one that shows the entire suspect, from head to toe, the interview room door, and the immediate vicinity around the suspect.[19] This camera angle allows the investigator to review the videotape for behavior symptom analysis and also clearly shows a judge or jury that there was no physical contact between the investigator and suspect. When evaluating a suspect's emotional state, or lack thereof, the court needs to be able to see and assess the suspect's posture, facial expressions and eye contact. The following photographs are a sample of different camera angles used in interview rooms at police departments,

---

[18] Despite the logic of this statement we did encounter some agencies who believed that if the entire interview room is not visible in the recording that the defense may argue that perhaps a second investigator, who was out of view, was making threatening gestures to the suspect which compelled him to confess. We did not run across a single instance where such a claim was made during a trial.

[19] A laboratory study determined that confessions were more likely to be perceived as voluntary if only the suspect was seen in the video. When the investigator was included within the recording, evaluators were more likely to believe coercion was involved. Lassiter, G.D., et al "Videotaped Interrogations and Confessions: A Simple Change in Camera Perspective Alters Verdicts in Simulated Trials." *Journal of Applied Psychology,* Vol. 87, No. 5 867-874, 2002.

along with our analysis.   The photos were recreated using our staff to protect the identity of the suspects and detectives in the original photographs.

The view in Camera Angle A shows the full suspect, his relationship to the door as well as the investigator.  In our opinion, this is an

excellent view for legal and investigative purposes.  A possible drawback to this view is if there was a second investigator present in the room, it does not show what that person is doing.

Camera Angle A

Camera Angle B is a standard overhead view of the interview room.  While it does show the position of all people in the room, it does not reveal any significant information about the suspect's nonverbal behavior.

Camera Angle B

Camera Angle C

Camera Angle C shows a fairly good frontal shot of the suspect (it would be nice to see all of the suspect's posture); however the investigator cannot be seen. In addition, it is not known where the suspect is sitting relative to the door.

Camera Angle D

Angle D is undesirable from all perspectives. The partially blocked view of the suspect does not document any key nonverbal behaviors (posture, facial expression, hand and leg movements). The view does not show what the investigator is doing, nor where the door is situated relative to the suspect. And Camera Angle E is excellent with respect to evaluating the suspect's nonverbal behavior and position relative to the door.

Camera Angle E

Camera Angle F

Angle F illustrates a picture-in-a-picture format. One angle shows a picture of the suspect's position (chair), which is excellent with respect to evaluating his nonverbal behavior while the other angle shows the entire room (upper right-hand corner of the caption). However neither angle shows where the door is in relation to the suspect or interrogator.

## Control Room

A control room has three areas with distinct purposes. The first area is for *live monitoring* of interviews or interrogations where other

investigators can follow the progress of an interrogation. The monitoring area in the caption can be channeled to view any of the four interview rooms. The microphone can be used to communicate with the interviewer during the interview via an earpiece worn by the interviewer. This will allow the interviewer to receive assistance from the observer without compromising the privacy of the room setting.

The second is a *playback area* where previously recorded

interviews and interrogations can be reviewed through the playback feature on the recorder after an interview has been completed. The tower in the caption contains four monitors, four VHS recorders, and four separate audio recorders allowing simultaneous recording of four interview rooms.

Finally, the control room should have a *dubbing area* where copies

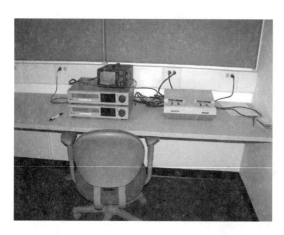

of the completed interview and interrogation can be produced. If the recording is digital it can be burned onto a DVD formatted disc. If analog tape was used, copies of the VHS and audiotapes can be produced with duplicating machines as illustrated in the photo. The subsequent discussion will describe how these functions are actually accomplished within the control room.

*Video*

The video signal will travel from the interview room to the control room via a wire, typically a coaxial cable. The video cable will connect to a primary recorder and possibly a backup, or redundant recorder and finally to a monitor. When the same cable connection is "looped" to a number of devices in this manner, some signal degradation will occur. To minimize this effect, it is recommended that the video cable initially be connected to a video distribution box which will split the original signal into three outputs of equal strength. This is to assure that the best quality video is being received by each component and it will also provide a fail-safe indicator – if there is no video on the monitor, there is no signal coming into the video distribution box. This assists troubleshooting in that the problem must be within the camera and not with any of the other components in the control room.

*Audio*

The audio signal entering the control room carries not only the conversation between the investigator and suspect, but additional room noise such as echoes and ambient noise from outside of the interview room. This excess sound can distort the conversations to an extent that portions of what was said in the room becomes indiscernible or inaudible. To eliminate or minimize extraneous sounds it is recommended that the audio signal first go through a voice processor. The voice processor accomplishes two important goals. First, it can eliminate much of the echo within the room and minimize outside noises. Second, the processor can control upper and lower volume thresholds. The lower level should be set to record a faint whisper while the upper level should be set slightly above conversational level. The threshold control makes certain that confessions offered in a quiet voice are still picked up and that the recording does not become distorted if there are raised voices in the room. The output from the processor should then be fed into an audio distribution box which will send a clean and amplified signal to recording devices and speakers.

*Recorders*

There are two standard mediums used to make electronic recordings, VHS (analog) and DVD (digital). All of our consultants agreed that digital recordings are superior to VHS. Although DVD is presently more costly than VHS, it provides a clearer video image. In addition, DVD has a number of other benefits over VHS recordings:

- Both visual and audio quality of DVD is considered to be nearly twice the resolution of VHS
- Unlike VHS, DVD quality will not deteriorate over time
- DVD recording capacity ranges from 1 - 12 hours
- DVD is more compact and easily stored
- DVD playback functions will allow investigators to play back portions of the interrogations while in progress and without interrupting the original recording
- DVD can be tabbed and reviewed much more quickly
- The digital format simplifies the electronic communication of video clips or still photos of a suspect to outside agencies for identification purposes
- It is estimated that manufacturers will discontinue making VHS players within the next 5-10 years, thus making VHS equipment obsolete.

The method of storage (analog, digital) will be the subject of scrutiny by defense attorneys and the courts. The videotape was the standard of audiovisual recording for many years and still has a faithful following. The practice of manipulating digital photographs is well publicized and the law enforcement agency must be able to assure a court of the integrity and authenticity of digital recordings. This begins by selecting a DVR (digital video recorder) that has a high level of encryption and also provides a watermark for additional security. These features make the information stored on the unit's hard drive unalterable. Several manufacturers have embedded hard drives and others will have a removable hard drive. This latter option may be desirable where there is a concern that the defense may subpoena the entire hard drive.

The DVR would then be fed to a DVD recorder which will record the data onto DVD-R formatted discs. Typically three discs are burned, the first for the investigator, the second for the prosecution and the third for the defense. If a department is reluctant to totally discontinue recording through a VHS medium, it is recommended that a simultaneous DVD recording be made to assure a safer and longer-lasting copy.

# Cost Estimates

The costs for electronically recording interviews and interrogations fall into two main categories. The first is the initial cost, which includes purchasing equipment and preparing the room for monitoring. The second include ongoing costs such as purchasing and storing recording tapes or disks, costs of maintaining equipment, personnel costs for making backup copies, transcripts, etc.

In making a financial decision concerning electronic recording there are cost savings to consider. While they may be difficult to quantify, there is a general belief that electronic recording results in more plea bargains and shorter trials. If this is the case, it may mean that a department can make more efficient use of their manpower since more of the officer's time will be spent enforcing laws and as opposed to waiting in court to testify.

When the Broward County Florida Sheriff's Office decided to implement a policy to videorecord interrogations, they conducted extensive research into a variety of issues, including the necessary equipment and associated costs. The department provided us with a copy of their itemized inventory that they felt was necessary to fully equip an average 8' x 10' interview room

| | |
|---|---|
| Sony SLV-N700 VHS VCR | $ 88.95 |
| AV400 AV distribution amp | $ 48.49 |
| Backup power supply | $175.00 |
| Super high gain micro audio system microphone | $ 12.95 |
| Visiontech AC-S 200 CPS.7 color board camera | $ 96.00 |
| Panasonic DMR-E55K DVD recorder | $360.00 |
| Tatung TCM-402S 14" monitor | $300.00 |
| 20" Television with composite video inputs | $175.00 |
| (20) Markerfoam 54"x54"x2" acoustical foam | $400.00 |
| (9 gallons) Tile mastic for adhesive | $ 69.00 |
| (4) 2"x4"x10" wood | $ 12.00 |
| (4) 1"x4"x10" white wood | $ 20.00 |

| | |
|---|---|
| (1) 1/4" lexan/acrylic sheet | $ 10.00 |
| (1) Door threshold | $ 15.00 |
| (1) Custom cabinet with doors | $ 120.00 |
| Misc tools/supplies/hardware | $ 100.00 |
| Floor mounted holding ring | $ 35.00 |
| (600) DVD-R media disks @ $2.00 | $1,200.00 |
| (200) VHS T-160 tapes @ 1.39 | $ 278.00 |

**TOTAL**            **$3,515.39**

# Storage

The investigator should treat the original electronic recording as any other piece of evidence with respect to preserving both the chain of evidence and the integrity of the evidence. Identifying information (case #, name, date, location) should be documented on both the tape or disk as well as the outside of the container. To protect the integrity of the recording, the following recommendations are made for storage:

- Breakaway recording tabs to prevent an original tape from being over-written
- Use a permanent marker felt-tip pen to identify each tape or disk
- Store tapes in a paper evidence bag to minimize condensation
- Do not store tapes or disks in extreme temperatures

- Avoid exposing tapes or disks to long periods of direct sunlight
- Avoid storing tapes or disks in areas of high humidity
- Do not store tapes or disks in dirty and dusty locations
- Protect analog recordings from electromagnetic fields (magnets, speakers, police radios, etc.)

# Recommendations

1. Audiovisual recording is preferable to audio recording alone.
2. Situate the interview/interrogation room away from noisy areas and insulate the walls.
3. Make audio recordings with a studio-quality powered microphone situated out of sight but near the suspect's chair.
4. A DVD visual recording is preferable to VHS. The camera should be positioned in a manner that the suspect is not constantly reminded that a recording is being made.
5. The best viewing angle is to have the camera show a full frontal view of the suspect (head, shoulders, torso and feet) as well as the interview room door.
6. There should be a means for investigators or others to monitor an interview or interrogation.
7. The electronic recordings should have a backup system in the event one recorder fails.
8. Three copies should be made of the electronically recorded interview interrogation.

9. The tape or disk containing the original recorded interview/interrogation should be identified and secured in an area that will preserve its integrity.

# Chapter 3

# INVESTIGATOR CONDUCT

Criminal interrogation requires knowledge in the areas of human behavior, psychology, persuasive communication and the law. While the courts have offered general guidelines regarding prohibited behaviors, a great deal of latitude is also provided to the interrogator, depending on a variety of circumstances. In real-life interrogations investigators may use vulgar language, may have physical contact with the suspect, may look at the suspect in an intimidating fashion, may make reference to a lighter sentence or intimate a possible harsher sentence, and even make reference to incriminating, sometimes fictitious, evidence against the suspect. Electronically recording interviews and interrogations will put the investigator's conduct on display. The thought of having every word and gesture examined by the judge, prosecuting attorney, defense attorney, and the jury is enough to make any investigator self-conscious about their conduct. It is true that some investigators will have to adjust their conduct during an interrogation now that they are being recorded. However, investigators who regularly practice legally acceptable interview and interrogation tactics have little to be concerned about.

Juries will see for the first time the tactics investigators use in real-life interrogations and will have the opportunity to evaluate the appropriateness of the tactics used by the interrogator. With the increasing popularity of 24-hour news channels, like Court TV, C-SPAN and COPS, jurors have become more sophisticated about the conduct of attorneys, judges, witnesses and defendants in the courtroom, the conduct of senators and representatives in senate and congressional hearings, and the conduct of police officers during an arrest of a suspect.

Cameras have shed light on the mystery behind a number of situations the general public was not privy to in the past and people have grown accustomed to having the opportunity to see the real-life situation and evaluate it based on their own perceptions. Investigators who have electronically recorded interrogations have found that if properly explained in court, juries are able to understand that sometimes the assertive interrogation techniques used by investigators are necessary to elicit the truth from a suspect.

In this chapter we will discuss the following areas of investigator conduct:

1. The Miranda warnings and waiver

2. Consent to electronically record

3. What to document during an interview/interrogation (Subject Data Sheet)

4. False statements by the interrogator

5. Jury perceptions of the investigator's conduct and interrogation tactics

6. Content of the confession

# Miranda Warnings and Waiver

The United States Supreme Court's 5-4 decision in *Miranda v. Arizona*,[20] established a specific requirement for confession admissibility. It was created so that all persons in police custody would know of the constitutional right against self-incrimination. The Court ruled that before a person in police custody or otherwise deprived of his freedom "in any significant way" could be interrogated, he must be given the following warnings:

1. You have the right to remain silent.
2. Anything you say can and will be used against you in a court of law.
3. You have the right to talk to a lawyer and to have him present with you while you are being questioned.
4. If you cannot afford to hire a lawyer, one will be appointed to represent you before any questioning, if you wish.

 After being advised of these rights the suspect must make a "knowing and intelligent" waiver before any questioning can take place.

Since the Minnesota law requiring the electronic recording of police interrogations went into effect in 1994 relatively few confessions have been suppressed. Those that have been suppressed have been primarily due to issues regarding Miranda as opposed to the interrogation process itself.[21] The issues that have been problematic are: whether the

---

[20] Miranda v. Arizona 384 U.S. 436 (1966)

[21] In our interviews with prosecutors they indicated that most of the confessions they have had suppressed were due in part to issues regarding Miranda, as opposed to the tactics used by the interrogator.

suspect was in custody, whether the suspect understood and clearly waived his Miranda rights, and whether the interrogator should have stopped when a suspect who initially waived his Miranda rights later made an ambiguous request for an attorney during the interrogation.    When electronically recording the interview and interrogation judges are afforded the opportunity to evaluate each of these issues and each case on its own merits. They no longer have to rely on the conflicting memories and statements of the investigator and the suspect.

*The appropriate time to advise the suspect of his Miranda rights*

Even though the U. S. Supreme court ruled that Miranda warnings are to be administered to a suspect in custody there appears to be an element of subjectivity when it comes to determining at what point an interview or interrogation becomes custodial.[22]

Investigators may face situations in which a non-custodial interview develops into a custodial interrogation because the suspect's incriminating statements represent probable cause, which the investigator acts on by taking the suspect into custody. The defense may argue that as soon as his client made incriminating statements, he should have been advised of his Miranda rights.    The prosecution may counter with their interpretation of the Supreme Court's opinion in Miranda that clearly indicates that once a non-custodial suspect has made an incriminating statement or has expressed a willingness to confess, he should be permitted without interruption to continue to make a full confession.    The interrogator

---

[22] Beckwith v. the United States, 425 U.S. 341  the court explicitly held that focus of suspicion was not the test as to whether the warnings are required; the test is whether the suspect is in custody.

should be able to ask questions at that time relating to the details of the crime without any legal impediment. After the suspect has related the details of the crime and before a written statement is taken, the suspect should be advised of his Miranda rights. It will then be left up to the court to resolve this legal question.

In November 2004, the Supreme Court of Tennessee ruled a videotaped confession inadmissible because the suspect was not advised of his Miranda rights when a non-custodial interview developed, in their opinion, into a custodial interrogation.[23] The case involved a fire at an apartment complex where the suspect and his elderly, bedridden mother lived. The mother was found dead in the apartment, but the cause of her death was initially unknown. After further investigation it was clear that the mother's death was not accidental. The investigators called the suspect and asked him to come to the police station to discuss the investigation. When the suspect arrived he was told that he was not under arrest and was escorted to an interview room just off the lobby.

The investigators conducted a non-accusatory interview followed by an accusatory interrogation. The interview was described by the court as a conversation between the suspect and investigators who discussed the victim's general condition and the events of the day the fire occurred. This discussion lasted approximately 35 minutes. The officers were described as polite and courteous and the suspect did not make any statements implicating himself in the fire or in his mother's death. The investigators stepped out of the interview room for a few minutes and returned shortly to

---

[23] State of TN v. William A. Payne, Jr. No. E2002-01307-SC-R11-CD.

begin the interrogation.

The court stated that during the interrogation, the "tone of this interview changed dramatically." The investigators "intensely" questioned the suspect in a "demanding and accusatory manor." The court also pointed out that one of the investigators was now sitting closer to the suspect, partially blocking his access to the door, whereas in the interview the investigator was sitting off to the side. The other investigator now stood near and somewhat over the suspect. The investigators denied the suspect's several requests to call his sister. During the interrogation, the suspect admitted that he accidentally hurt his mother's neck while trying to help her. When he realized that he had injured her, he set her bed on fire and fled the scene, returning to work. The court determined that it was at this point that the non-custodial interview turned custodial and the incriminating statements made by the suspect made were inadmissible. The court concluded:

> *"...a reasonable person in the defendant's position would have considered himself deprived of freedom of movement to a degree associated with a formal arrest at least when the interview resumed after the first break . At this point, the demeanor, tone, and questioning markedly changed, as did the officers' physical locations in the room."*

This case reinforces the principle that custody can be inferred through the totality of circumstances. However, since diverse courts may view similar situations very differently, the investigator is left with ambiguous guidelines as to when a non-custodial interview turns into a custodial interrogation. As a result, in some jurisdictions the investigators overcome this by advising a suspect of his Miranda rights prior to the initial interview even though there is no probable cause to place the suspect in custody. If the suspect waives his rights and agrees to talk to the investigators without an attorney present, the investigator does not have to reissue Miranda warnings if the interview moves into a custodial interrogation.

*The appropriate language of Miranda warnings*

Advising a suspect of his Miranda rights has become second nature for most experienced investigators who know the warnings by rote. Even though the Supreme Court held in 1981 that there was no requirement for the Miranda warnings to be a "virtual incantation of the precise language contained in Miranda" investigators should exercise caution when straying from the precise language, as illustrated in the following electronically recorded examples:

> *"You have the right to remain silent and anything you say can be used <u>for</u> or against you."*

> *"You have the right to remain silent, and I think you ought to use it."*

While these improvisations did not cause either of the confessions to be suppressed, it did result in extensive arguments before the judge.[24]

---

[24] Anecdotes related during our interviews with prosecuting attorneys.

*Suspects ambiguous request for an attorney*

One of the most challenging and difficult Miranda issues that investigators encounter during an interrogation is when the suspect makes an ambiguous request for an attorney or mentions the word lawyer, such as "I wonder if I should have an attorney?" or "Maybe I need a lawyer" or "I would like a lawyer, but it wouldn't do any good." The U.S. Supreme Court held in *Davis v. United States*, (1994)[25] that unless the suspect clearly and unambiguously asserts his right to counsel, police do not have to stop questioning the suspect or even ask for clarification. In this case the suspect said, "Maybe I should talk to a lawyer." The investigators did clarify this statement by asking the suspect whether he wanted a lawyer or not. The suspect said he did not and his subsequent incriminating statements were admitted in as evidence.

Some states, for example Minnesota, require police to ask clarifying questions of any such request, and it is the recommendation of the authors that all investigators clarify any request of a suspect regarding an attorney during a custodial interrogation. This is particularly prudent when electronically recording the interrogation because if the request, no matter how ambiguous, is ignored by the interrogator it may serve as the basis for an effective challenge by the defense. An effective way for investigators to handle a request for a lawyer is to ask the suspect, "It's up to you; do you want a lawyer or not?" or "I read you your rights, and whether you want an attorney, is entirely up to you. Would you like me to read your rights to you again?" If the suspect declines to have his rights

---

[25] Davis v. United States 512 U.S. 452 (1994).

read again and agrees to talk without an attorney then the interrogation can proceed. However, if the suspect clearly states that he does not want to talk any further without his attorney present the interrogation must stop at this point.[26]

*Documenting the suspect's understanding of his Miranda rights and establishing a voluntary waiver*

In addition to advising the suspect of his Miranda rights at the proper time, investigators have to guard against speaking too fast or mumbling as they are going through this familiar routine. Investigators should speak slowly and clearly to the suspect and elicit a verbal waiver from the suspect as opposed to just a simple nod of the head. This is particularly important when only an audio recording of the warnings is being made.

Extra care should be taken with some juvenile offenders, individuals who are mentally or cognitively impaired, under the influence of alcohol or drugs at the time of questioning, or individuals with a limited understanding of the language to be sure that they understand their rights. Under these circumstances we recommend that after advising the suspect of each right, the investigator should ask the suspect to explain what the right means to him, e.g., "You have the right to remain silent. What does that mean to you?" This extra effort may mean the difference between a confession that is admitted versus one that is suppressed. Consider the following case:

---

[26] For a more detailed discussion of this issue and others regarding Miranda see Criminal Interrogations and Confessions 4th Edition by Inbau, F. Reid, J. Buckley, J & Jayne, B. pages 489-521.

*The People v. Javier H. (2004) Cal. No. A103020*

In this case the juvenile court found Javier H. guilty of murder and attempted robbery of a 55-year-old immigrant from El Salvador. An argument was made to the court that Javier was not competent to understand his Miranda rights and was inclined to want to please adults and be agreeable toward authority figures. The McArthur competency assessment test was administered to Javier which indicated that he had "low abstraction ability" which might make it difficult for him to understand legal concepts. The court was advised that the defendant "has a history of wanting to please adults... he wants people to praise him, to like him, to be on his side." It was suggested that the defendant might be even less likely to admit he didn't understand something when talking to the police than to other adults.

The judge reviewed the video and audiotape of the interviews investigators conducted with Javier and stated:

> *"I was impressed as I watched the tapes that the officers did carefully, on each occasion where it was recorded on the tape, slowly explain the rights, in the sense that they asked the questions that they're required to ask. And on each occasion, asked Javier if he understood that, and on each occasion, they insisted on a yes or yeah audible answer... This was a young man who knew what he was doing, at least in my opinion. That's the evidence I have... and he knew that when he was getting into an area where he was getting tripped up, he knew enough to become vague... I'm going to find, therefore, that Javier did make a knowing, intelligent and voluntary waiver of his rights without any compulsion or any reward of leniency that I can see or hear on the tapes."*

When investigators electronically record a non-custodial interview they should make it clear on the tape that the suspect is not under arrest and is free to leave. To further establish the non-custodial nature of the interview, investigators should leave the suspect in the interview room alone with the door unlocked or allow the suspect to leave the room unescorted to use the restroom or get a drink of water. During a non-custodial interview or interrogation, the investigator should not confiscate the suspect's cell phone. If the investigator initiates a non-custodial interrogation he should periodically remind the suspect that he is not under arrest and is free to leave at any time. Any incriminating statements the suspect makes during this non-custodial interrogation should be admissible even though the Miranda warnings were not administered.

# Proper Release Forms and Subject Data Sheet

*The importance of the Subject Data Sheet*

The defense may attempt to discredit the integrity of the confession by suggesting that the defendant was not emotionally or physiologically able to withstand the stress of a police interrogation. In other circumstances it may be claimed that the defendant was incapable of understanding what the interrogators were saying to him. Finally, the attorney may argue that the defendant was fatigued, not feeling well, was under the influence of alcohol, illegal drugs or prescription medication at the time of the interrogation.

To prepare for these types of arguments, investigators should ask

---

27 Oregon v. Mathiason, 429 U.S. 492 (1977).

the following questions in the early stages of the interview in an effort to establish whether the suspect's emotional, psychological, and physical well-being is suitable for an interrogation.

In the last 24 hours, have you had any alcohol, drugs or medication?

In the last 24 hours, how many hours of sleep have you had?

How long ago did you eat your last full meal?

What was the last year of school you completed?

Are you presently experiencing any physical discomfort?

Are you presently under a physician's care for any medical problem?

In the last 12 months, have you talked to a psychologist or psychiatrist about an emotional or mental-health problem?

How would you describe your present physical well-being?

The suspect's answers to these questions will allow a judge to objectively evaluate the suspect's suitability for an interrogation, as illustrated in the earlier-mentioned Javier case.

An alternative method of developing this information is to have the suspect complete a data sheet at the outset of the interview. This will document, in the suspect's own handwriting, his suitability for an interrogation. An example of a data sheet suitable for this purpose can be found in Appendix F.

### *Advising the suspect that he is being electronically recorded*

A common concern investigators and prosecutors have voiced about electronically recording interrogations is that it may make suspects less likely to tell the truth. Research supporting this concern was covered in Chapter one. Specifically, investigators had a higher confession rate when the recording device was not visible to the suspect. A logical extension of this finding is that notifying a suspect that an interview is being electronically recorded may cause the suspect to be less forthright.

Several states' eavesdropping statutes require two-party consent to record a conversation.[28] Absent a law enforcement exemption, under this circumstance, the investigator must obtain the suspect's permission to electronically record. In states with a one-part consent, the investigator need not notify the suspect that a recording is being made. Even under this circumstance, some states attorneys may still instruct investigators to inform suspects that they are being recorded. It is up to the investigator to review this issue with their state's attorney to determine whether suspects should be advised that they are being electronically recorded and determine what type of consent (oral or written) is preferred.

If the suspect's permission is not legally required to electronically record the interview, does the investigator have a responsibility to be

---

[28] A list of State Eavesdropping laws can be found in Appendix H.

truthful with the suspect if asked whether or not a recording is being made? In our interviews with prosecuting attorneys we were informed that as long as the investigator has identified himself as a police officer, or while they are in the police department, the suspect has no "expectation of privacy." Therefore the investigator is not required to inform the suspect they are being recorded even if the suspect asks. However, if the investigator lies to the suspect about being electronically recorded this will have to be addressed in court. As one prosecuting attorney explained, "I simply tell the judge and jury that the reason the officer lied about taping was to create a more relaxed atmosphere for the suspect and to prevent the suspect from playing to the camera." In essence it was for the suspect's own benefit. The prosecutor also points out that this will allow the court to review a more accurate and sincere representation of the suspect's statements and demeanor. However, prosecutors we spoke to encouraged police officers to be honest with the suspect if they are asked whether or not the conversation is being recorded. Another means some law enforcement agencies use to advise the public that they should have "no expectation of privacy" while in the station house is to post signs at each entrance informing those who enter that they may be monitored. (Photo 3-A)

Photo 3-A

*For security purposes, premises are monitored by audio and visual equipment.*

*Por razones de seguridad este lugar esta vigilado por medio de equipo audio visual*

If the investigator is required to get consent to electronically record the interview he can either have the suspect sign a written release form or elicit oral consent from the suspect on tape. (For an an example of a written release form consenting to electronic recording, see Appendix G.)

In states that require electronic recording, the suspect has the right to request that the tape be turned off during their interview or interrogation. If the suspect makes such a request, the investigator should clearly document, on tape, that the suspect made the request to stop recording. If this is not done, any subsequent statements the suspect makes may be inadmissible.

# Documentation

*Investigator notes during the interview*

As prescribed later in this book investigators should take written notes during the course of the interview even though the interview is being electronically recorded. These notes should be limited to objective observations and avoid any comments that indicate a subjective interpretation of a suspect's verbal or non-verbal behavior, e.g., truthful or deceptive. A good rule to follow is that investigators should avoid writing anything in their notes that they would not feel comfortable sharing with or explaining to a defense attorney.

If more than one investigator is taking notes, the two sets of notes should be reviewed for consistency immediately following the interview and interrogation. A defense attorney will look for any opportunity to point out inconsistencies between the two investigators. If discrepancies are found, it may be argued that there was a conspiracy against his client or gross incompetence on the part of the investigators

One of the advantages of electronically recording a suspect's interview and interrogation is that it will greatly assist in refreshing the investigator's memory and help prepare for trial. Especially in a serious crime, the trial may take place many months after the interview and interrogation of the suspect and the investigator must rely on his notes and the electronic recording to recall pertinent details.

Here is a general guideline of the types of information that should be documented during note-taking:

a. Were Miranda rights administered to the suspect? If so, when were they administered and by whom? How did the suspect indicate that he understood his rights and waived them?

b. Did the suspect request an attorney or say he no longer wanted to answer any questions during the interview or interrogation? If so, when did this occur and how was the request handled?

c. If Miranda rights were not given, was the suspect advised that he was not under arrest and free to leave? If so, when and how many times was the suspect advised that he was free to leave? Did the suspect ask to leave? If so, was the suspect allowed to leave? What time was he allowed to do so?

d. Was an interpreter used in the interview? If so, identify the interpreter and their relationship to the investigation or suspect.

e. What time did the interview begin and end? Document the times of any breaks taken during the interview and the reason for the breaks.

f. Was the suspect offered anything to eat, or drink? If so, when did this occur and what was provided to the suspect?

g. What were the suspect's statements regarding their physical, emotional, and psychological condition at the time of the interrogation? Refer to the Subject Data Sheet.

h. Who was in the interrogation room with the suspect? Document the times and reason other individuals may have been in the room.

i. What was the primary theme used during the interrogation?

j. What Alternative question did the suspect confess to?

k. What time did the suspect make their first admission of guilt?

l. What time did the suspect begin to give a formal statement?

m. What was the suspect's demeanor during his confession?

n. Who witnessed the confession?

# What Should Be Electronically Recorded

There are two considerations with respect to what should be electronically recorded. The first relates to the type of case (felony, crimes against person, custodial, etc.) and the second is what portions of the interaction with a suspect should be electronically recorded. These options range from only recording the confession or only the interview, to recording the entire period of time a suspect is in the room, including when he is alone in the room.

There is currently no federal legislation that requires or regulates the electronic recording of custodial interviews and interrogations. States that have passed legislation requiring law enforcement to electronically record interviews have established their own guidelines regulating the process. Alaska[29] and Minnesota,[30] for example, require investigators to electronically record all custodial interrogations conducted in a *place of detention* while Illinois[31] only requires the electronic recording of the custodial interrogations of persons accused in homicide investigations

---

[29] Stephan v. State, 711 P.2d 1156, 1158 Alaska 1985.

[30] State v. Scales, 518 N.W. 2d 587 Minn, 1994; states; *"All custodial interrogation including any information about rights, any waiver of those rights, and all questioning shall be electronically recorded where feasible and must be recorded when questioning takes place at a place of detention... If law enforcement officers fail to comply with this requirement, then statements the suspect makes in response to the interrogation may be suppressed at trial... Suppression will be required if the violation is deemed 'substantial.'*

[31] Public Act 93-0206, HB 223, Illinois 2005.

while *in a place of detention*, and New Jersey[32] only requires investigators to electronically record a suspect's confession and not the entire interview and interrogation.

### Electronically recorded confessions

In jurisdictions where investigators are not required to electronically record the complete interrogation they may only record the confession. This practice opens the door for the defense to argue that because the investigator had the capability to record the confession he should have also recorded the complete interrogation. The defense may suggest that the reason the investigator did not record the complete interrogation was because there must have been something that was done or said that the investigator did not want the judge or jury to see.

If electronically recording only the confession, investigators should be sure to repeat the Miranda warnings to the suspect even though they were issued prior to the custodial interrogation, referencing the fact that the suspect had received and waived them earlier. In cases where the complete interrogation has been electronically recorded this may seem unnecessary because the issuance of Miranda has already been recorded. However, this incorporation of the warnings in the confession will provide evidence that the waiver was a continuing one up to the time of the confession.

### Benefits of Continuous Electronic Recording

States that require electronic recording mandate that the recording

---

[32] Attorney General Peter C. Harvey, Jan 2005, expanded and made permanent a policy directing police departments and prosecutors to electronically record confessions in criminal cases.

begin as soon as the suspect is placed in the interrogation room or in a *place of detention*. Continuous electronic recording from that point on may not be required but the Miranda waiver, the entire interrogation and any statements made by the suspect while in the interrogation room must be recorded to satisfy admissibility requirements.[33]

Another option is to continuously record the suspect while he is in the interrogation room. This literally means that the recorder is turned on from the time the suspect enters the room and is not turned off until the suspect permanently leaves the room. There are a several advantages to adopting a policy where suspects are continuously recorded.

There are numerous anecdotes of suspects making incriminating statements or acting in an incriminating manner while alone in the interrogation room. For example, in one case a suspect who was pretending to be legally blind began reading when the investigators left the room. In another case, after making repeated denials that he raped and stabbed the victim to death, when left alone in the room the suspect was recorded singing, "Ding, dong, the wicked witch is dead..." In a case from the Chicago area, the suspect, while alone in the interrogation room, is seen on videotape slamming his head against the concrete wall in an effort to cause visual trauma which, had it not been for the videotape, would have been blamed on the interrogator.

Some suspects are a little more savvy and may try to use the

---

[33] As with many legal decisions there are exceptions or circumstances that occur where the courts may allow into evidence unrecorded incriminating statements made by a custodial suspect. One such circumstance may be when the suspect himself requests that his statements not be recorded. Another may be when the investigator can make a "reasonable explanation" to the court that it was not *feasible* to record the suspect's statements. However, if the court considers the investigator's actions an "unexcused failure to record," suspect's unrecorded statements may be suppressed. A list of *acceptable exemptions* established in Illinois HB concerning electronic recording can be found in the Appendix C.

electronic recording  as an opportunity to play to the judge or jury.  While alone in the room they may talk to themselves saying, "I can't believe they think I did this."  "This is crazy; they have no right to accuse me of something like this."  "I can't believe they made me confess to something I didn't do."

*Officer safety* is another reason to continuously record a suspect while alone in the interrogation room.  This was dramatically illustrated in a rare and unusual circumstance in California when a 47-year-old suspect pulled out a gun and shot himself after the interrogator left the room briefly to talk to another detective.  The suspect had been stopped for a traffic violation and fled the scene in his car and later on foot.  During the chase the suspect shot one of the pursuing officers twice in the abdomen.  The suspect was arrested and brought to the sheriff's headquarters and placed in an interrogation room.  Somehow the suspect had the gun hidden on his body and it was not discovered during his arrest.  After the suspect shot himself, the returning detective can be heard on the tape saying, "Nobody shook him (searched him for weapons)."

It was initially theorized that the suspect may have been executed.  However, the videotape clearly showed the suspect alone in the room.  He calmly took the revolver out of his pocket, placed it to this head, and shot himself.  This graphic video has since been used in Police Officer Safety training programs and has been posted on the internet.

Electronically recording the complete interrogation exposes some suspects for who they really are and allows the judge and jury to see the suspect in a more accurate light.  In the courtroom the suspect may appear to be polite, well-groomed, and well-mannered.  However, during the interrogation the jury may see the suspect spewing insults and vulgarities at the investigators and expressing no remorse regarding their actions. This may be quite contrary to the image the suspect is now trying to portray in the courtroom.

# Statements Made to a Suspect by the Interrogator

*False statements made by the investigator*

*Case Law*

Courts appreciate the fact that on some occasions investigators must rely on pretense and innuendo in an effort to obtain evidence against a guilty suspect. The landmark decision supporting the use of trickery and deceit, *Frazier v. Cupp*, involves a case in which the police falsely told a homicide suspect that his accomplice had already confessed to the crime.[34] The U.S. Supreme Court stated that:

> *"The fact that the police misrepresented the statements that [the suspected accomplice] had made is, while relevant, insufficient in our view to make this otherwise voluntary confession inadmissible. These cases must be decided by viewing the "totality of circumstances..."*

In 1981 the Supreme Court of Canada ruled that the deceptive actions of the investigator had not rendered inadmissible the information that he had obtained. In a concurring opinion Justice Antonio Lamer stated:

---

[34] Frazier v. Cupp, 394 U.S. 731, 89 S. Ct. 1420 (1969).

> *"There is nothing inherently wrong in outsmarting criminals into admitting their guilt or into jeopardizing the liberty they might be tempted to take with the truth in the course of their trial... It must also be borne in mind... that the investigation of crime and the detection of criminals is not a game to be governed by the Marquess of Queensbury rules."*[35]

Justice Lamer recognized the fact that the police "must sometimes of necessity resort to tricks or other forms of deceit." He did caution, however, that the trickery and deceit should not be of such nature as to "shock the community," such as the investigator posing as a clergyman or defense attorney in an effort to obtain a confession.

In a 1993 decision, a state supreme court used the test of "intrinsic vs. extrinsic" deception in upholding a suspect's confession to rape.[36] Under this test the court ruled that "employment by police of deliberate falsehoods intrinsic to the facts of the alleged offense in question will be treated as one of the totality of circumstances... in assessing... voluntariness." Conversely, deliberate falsehoods extrinsic to the facts of the alleged offense would be regarded as coercive per se. In this particular case, the police lied to the suspect by telling him that medical evidence revealed evidence of rape, which was intrinsic to the facts of the offense. An example of an extrinsic false statement that would not be permissible during an interrogation would be lying to a suspect about the possible sentence he faces, e.g., "This is your lucky day. Last week the legislature reduced first- degree murder down to a misdemeanor."

Twenty years following Frazier, another significant case, *State v.*

---

[35] Rothman v. the Queen, 59 C.C.C.2d 30 (1981).

[36] State v. Kelekolio, 849 P 2d 58 , Hawaii (1993).

*Cayward*, further clarified the extent to which an investigator can engage in trickery or deceit.[37] To persuade a suspect in a sexual homicide to confess, police typed up a fictitious crime laboratory report which indicated that the suspect's DNA had been found on the victim. After reading this fabricated report, the suspect confessed. The court suppressed the suspect's confession, not out of concern that the fabricated report would cause an innocent person to confess, but rather that manufacturing evidence in this manner threatens a loss of integrity within the judicial system. The case law that comes out of Cayward is that a distinction must be made between false verbal assertions (which may be permissible) and manufacturing evidence (which is impermissible).

The guideline offered in Cayward has been used in a number of cases to suppress confessions under circumstances where the investigator manufactured evidence. Examples include a fabricated crime lab report indicating that the suspect's DNA was found on a rubber glove recovered at the crime scene[38] and a fabricated audiotape in which an investigator played the role of an eyewitness to the suspect's crime, while another investigator questioned him.[39] The prohibition against manufacturing fictitious evidence should in no way prevent an investigator from using visual props during an interrogation, provided, of course, that the props would never be misinterpreted as actual evidence against the suspect in a court of law.

*Recommendations*

An investigator must balance the wide latitude that the courts afford

---

[37] State v. Cayward, 552 So 2d. at 974.

[38] State v. Chirokovskcic, 373 N.J. Super. 125 (App. Div., 2004).

[39] State v. Patton 826 A.2d 783, N.J.Super.A.D., 2003.

the use of false statements made during an interrogation (in an effort to learn the truth) against the jury's perception of taking unfair advantage of the defendant through unethical and deceptive practices. The emotional side of this issue should not be minimized, as there are a number of influential writers who strongly believe that trickery and deceit should be strictly prohibited during an interview or interrogation.[40] As a guideline, we believe that any false statement made to a suspect should be defensible in that the investigator can articulate to the court why the false statement was made. Examples of possible explanations are discussed in Chapter 5.

*Statements that imply a promise of leniency to the suspect*

Electronically recording interviews and interrogations places additional demands on investigators to choose their words carefully. It may be tempting for an investigator to tell a suspect during the interrogation that he wants to "help" the suspect in some way. However, some courts have ruled that expressing a willingness to help the suspect constitutes an implied promise of leniency. A similar ruling may occur by telling the suspect that, "It would be better if you confessed" or, "The best thing you can do is to confess." Other examples of phrases that may imply a promise of leniency, and therefore should be avoided, include:

> *"I want to help you out on this."*
>
> *"I'll tell the prosecutor you cooperated and work out a deal for you."*

---

[40] See "The Ethics of Deceptive Interrogation" by Skolnik, J. & Leo, R. In Issues in Policing New Perspectives, (J. Bizzack ed,) 1992; Kamisar, Y. Police Interrogation and Confessions, University of Michigan Press, 1980.

*"I think you will just go into treatment for this, don't worry about jail."*

*"It would be better if you told me truth about this."*

*"It would be best if you explained your involvement in this."*

As one prosecutor explained, investigators can avoid this by carefully choosing their words during the interrogation. Instead of saying "I want to help you out on this" or "It would be better if you told me the truth about this" the investigator should say;

*"I want to give you a chance to tell the truth about this."*

*"I want to give you an opportunity to explain your side of this."*

*"Don't you think it would be important for you to tell the truth about this."*

*"I think it would be important for people to understand how this happened, don't you?"*

These statements still portray the investigator's interest and concern for the suspect but avoid implying a promise of leniency to the suspect.

If the suspect asks the investigator, "What will happen to me if I say I did this?" the investigator should respond by telling the suspect, "That's not up to me, I can't promise you anything; the important thing for you to do is to tell the truth so the people who are making those decisions can make a fair assessment of your case."

During the course of an interrogation the investigator may slip up and make a statement that could be construed as an implied promise of leniency. Under this circumstance a *prophylactic statement* may negate the damaging effects of the statement. A *prophylactic statement* is designed to prevent the possible misinterpretation of a previous statement. The following is an example of a prophylactic statement that cancels a possible implied promise of leniency:

- Possible promise of leniency

  "Jim, all I'm saying is that if this is something that was out of character for you because you have a problem with alcohol. That is something that can be handled through treatment."

- Prophylactic Statement

  "Now understand what I'm saying. I'm not saying if you did this you will not do some time, I'm just saying that if you get this straightened out, you can get treatment for your drinking problem."

*Statements that imply a threat to the suspect*

Investigators should also refrain from using any statements that may convey a *threat* to the suspect. For example, during the interrogation of a suspect in an auto theft investigation, the investigator was recorded telling the suspect that, "If you're hiding anything from us you're "really going to get hammered."[41] This statement was productive in eliciting a confession from the suspect. However, the court concluded that the

---

[41] Beavers v. State, 998 P.2d 1040, 1044-48 (Alaska 2000).

investigator's statement constituted a threat of harsher treatment if the suspect did not confess. They concluded that such a threat rendered the resulting *"statement presumptively involuntary absent evidence affirmatively establishing that the suspect's will was not overborne by the threat."*

As these examples illustrate, even if there is no evidence that the investigator physically mistreated the suspect or deprived him of biological needs, the investigator's words can imply a threat of physical harm and contribute to a decision to suppress a confession.

*Threats of inevitable consequences*

Another type of threat that can nullify a confession is one that threatens inevitable consequences. Under this circumstance the suspect is told that regardless of their denials and stated innocence, they will still suffer consequences. Furthermore, the suspect's only hope at reducing the consequence is to confess.

Examples of statements which threaten an inevitable consequence include, "If you don't confess your kids will be put in a foster home and you will never see them again!" or, "There is not a judge or jury in this country who will believe you. You're going to prison. The only question is how long."

# Jury Perceptions of the Investigator's Conduct

Eliciting a legally acceptable voluntary confession from a suspect can pose a significant challenge to any investigator. Suspects generally approach the interview with the perception that the investigator's objective is to get them to confess to the crime they committed so they can be prosecuted and punished. Consequently, guilty suspects are highly motivated to do whatever is possible to successfully deceive the investigator and avoid making any incriminating statements.

To be successful in their goal, investigators must develop a rapport with the suspect, gain that person's trust, and apply techniques of active persuasion in an effort to elicit a legally admissible confession. This is a daunting task and one that sometimes requires the use of unsavory and unethical tactics as illustrated by the following comments:

> *"There are certain things that the U.S. Supreme Court has said are all right to do in an investigation... it's OK to lie to a defendant to test their story... but that's something that might be hard for a jury to see on a tape and understand."*        *(Assistant States Attorney)*

> *"The things police do may be legal, but they shock most people. They see the yelling, the intimidation. To the average person, this tends to be a revelation."*
> *(Retired Broward County Police Officer)*

In an effort to learn the truth, investigators often have to empathize with a suspect and give the appearance that they are taking their side. The investigator may offer psychological justifications for the suspect's actions and even shift the blame for the suspect's actions onto the victim of the crime in their effort to learn the truth. Suspects may become challenging during the interrogation and strongly deny any knowledge or involvement in the crime under investigation. Deceptive suspects may feign a number of emotions in their effort to avoid telling the truth, including displays of shock, humiliation or anger. To maintain control of the interrogation, the investigator may have to feign annoyance by raising his voice, or employ psychological manipulation such as avoiding eye contact or leaning closer to the suspect. Some criminal suspects remain totally unaffected by conventional persuasion. Under this circumstance it may be appropriate for the investigator to engage in profanity, stand over the suspect and assume a tone of voice and facial expressions that could be described as hostile. Naturally, an investigator should be concerned about a judge or jury's perception of such tactics and carefully consider the suspect's age, intelligence, attitude, and prior experience with the criminal justice system.

As stated earlier, investigators and prosecutors who have experience using electronically recorded interrogations have found that juries have become quite sophisticated about police tactics and, as long as the investigator and prosecutor explain the tactics in court, juries are willing to tolerate the use of certain unsavory tactics to elicit the truth from a suspect.

*The seriousness of the crime may affect a jury's tolerance of interrogation tactics*

Sometimes the investigator's actions, although extreme, need no explanation. Consider the following case example related to one of the authors by a prosecuting attorney with 30 years of experience. The prosecutor presented an audiotape to the court of an interrogation where it sounded like the interrogator lunged across the table and grabbed the suspect by the shirt. However, the tape did not reveal any indications of the investigator physically striking the suspect. The suspect was being interrogated regarding the assault and murder of an 88-year-old woman who just recently had hip replacement surgery. The crime scene revealed that after the woman was attacked, she was left  in the back of (the defendant's) van where she froze to death. The prosecutor reported  that the jury did not have any problem with the physical treatment of the suspect given the serious nature of the crime.  They could empathize with the investigator's emotional state at the time of the interrogation  and found the suspect guilty.

As a general rule, prosecutors have found that the more serious the jury perceives the defendant's crime, the more forgiving they are toward aggressive or lengthy interrogations.  Of course there are limits to the tolerance of any judge or jury.  Consider a case involving a 50-hour interrogation of a mildly retarded 25-year-old juvenile who was allegedly beaten by investigators in an effort to elicit a confession.  Despite the fact that the crime under investigation was a homicide, the totality of circumstances in this case goes beyond what any reasonable person would find acceptable.[42]  The electronically recorded confession in this case was preceeded by a 50-hour unrecorded interrogation.  The court had to rely on the conflicting statements of the defendant and the investigators to determine what occurred during the interrogation.

---

[42] A mildly retarded 25-year-old man falsely confessed on videotape to killing his mother in July 2000, after a 50-hour unrecorded interrogation.  Bell alleged in court documents that the reason he confessed was because the police hit him so hard that he was knocked off his chair.  He said he felt hopeless and worn down after being in custody for more that two days.  He said he thought that once he had a chance to go before a judge he could explain that he was innocent and be released.  DNA evidence was later used to identify the actual killer and Bell was released after spending 17 months in jail.

*Lengthy interrogations*

The length of an interrogation can influence the perception of the voluntariness of the confession and also test the patience of the jury. However, a lengthy interrogation does not necessarily mean that a court will consider the confession coerced or involuntary, as illustrated in the following case. A homicide suspect confessed to murder and argued that his confession should be suppressed because he was coerced into making the incriminating statements. The suspect alleged that he was subjected to 20 hours of interrogation by (the) investigators who "feigned empathy, flattery, and engaged in lengthy discourse…" Fortunately the entire 20 hours of interrogation over six days was videotaped.

After reviewing the tapes, the court observed that the defendant was repeatedly advised of his Miranda rights, that the sessions were initiated by the defendant, that the sessions were not individually lengthy, and that the defendant was given refreshments, food, and breaks during the sessions. The court concluded that *"The tapes show that the confession was entirely voluntary under the Fifth Amendment and that no improper coercion was employed."*[43]

If an interrogation is too lengthy jurors may become bored and it could slow down the momentum of the trial. Some juries are anxious to get to the bottom of things and may find it tedious to listen to hours of tape that may be rambling in content (incoherent) or contain extraneous information. Investigators can help to avoid this problem by coming into the interview organized, with a clear understanding of the information they need to

---

[43] Owen v. State, 862 So. 2d 687 Fla., Oct. 2003.

develop from the suspect. Understanding the legal nature of the offense, the way the crime appears to have been committed, the details of its commission, possible motives, and any incriminating factors against the suspect will help in the development of questions to be asked in the interview. This will allow the investigator to keep the interview on track and help reduce the amount of extraneous information elicited during an unstructured interview.

The same level of preparation should precede the interrogation of a suspect. Prior to an interrogation the investigator should decide how best to confront the suspect, whether to use a factual or emotional interrogation approach, what themes may be suggested, what possible evidence could be used during the interrogation, and what alternative question is most likely to elicit the first admission of guilt.

*Written transcripts are provided to juries*

In addition to developing an interrogation strategy likely to persuade a suspect to confess, when an interrogation is being electronically recorded the investigator must also anticipate how his interrogation will be viewed by a jury. To help the jury follow along with the tape and clearly understand what is being said, a transcript of the interrogation is typically prepared. In some jurisdictions the jury is instructed that the transcript is to be used only to assist in understanding the tape and it is not to be considered as evidence. Furthermore, if there is any discrepancy between the tape and the transcript, the jury is instructed to evaluate what was said on the tape. In an effort to keep the jury's interest while listening to a lengthy audiotape of an interview or interrogation, some prosecutors will stop the tape periodically and have the investigator describe what the suspect was doing nonverbally during that particular time. For example, during a non-custodial interview of a suspect who was accused of sexual assault there was a squeaking noise that could be heard on the tape. The defense attorney had been arguing that his client was in custody and should have been read his Miranda rights. It was claimed that his client was under duress and was being badgered by the investigator. The prosecuting attorney stopped the tape at the point the squeaking noise was heard and asked the investigator what was causing the noise. The investigator explained that was the sound of the suspect's chair as the suspect moved his own chair closer to the investigator. While listening to the tape the judge stated that, "This is the most amicable conversation I have heard between a suspect and investigator" and ruled that Miranda was not necessary and admitted the suspect's statements as evidence.

*Electronically recorded interviews and interrogations are edited for the courtroom*

In most cases the taped interview and interrogation is not played for the jury in its entirety. Often, the only sections of the tape that may be played to the jury are those agreed upon by the prosecuting attorney, the defense attorney and the judge. If the suspect makes any statements concerning past criminal behavior or statements that may prejudice the jury, the court is likely to edit out that information from the tape. For example, a suspect may make reference to a person he served time with in prison or his involvement in some past criminal behavior. A judge may rule that these references cannot be played for the jury. There is also an effort to avoid playing any statement out of context by either the suspect or the interrogator. The judge, prosecuting and defense attorneys will stipulate what sections of the tape will be shown to the jury. The tape is then edited for courtroom play.

*Repeated viewing and camera angle may affect jurors' perception of the electronically recorded interview and interrogation*

Prosecutors have found that even when jurors are listening to or watching the same tape they may have different impressions of the suspect and the interrogator. One prosecuting attorney explained that he played a tape of an interview of a female child who was sexually abused. The victim made the allegations of sexual abuse on the tape but refused to make those same statements in court. This gave the defense attorney the opportunity to attack the taped interview of the child as being unreliable, indicating that the investigator suggested to her what she should say. The jury was shown the tape in court but was not allowed to take it with them during deliberations. If the jury wanted to see the tape again they were allowed to do so but they were not permitted to watch the tape over and over during deliberations. In this case, the one juror who thought the interview was suggestive after the first viewing didn't think the interview was suggestive at all after viewing it a second time. However, another juror had the opposite reaction. She thought the interview was very suggestive after watching it a second time.

Studies have shown that there is a correlation between a jury's assessment of a statement's voluntariness and the focus angle of the videocamera. A suspect's statement was viewed as voluntary more often when the camera angle focused on the suspect alone (subject focus) as compared to when the camera angle showed both the suspect and the interrogator (equal-focus).[44] In another study the conviction rate doubled when the tape was changed from an equal-focused view to a suspect-focused view.[45] Some prosecuting attorneys prefer that the camera angle focus on the suspect and have never heard any objection from a judge or a jury that the investigator was not shown during the interrogation. The most important consideration is that statements made by both the investigator and suspect are understandable and audible.

Not surprisingly, prosecutors have found that since the requirement for electronic recording of interviews and interrogations, there has been a decrease in the use of vulgarities, physical intimidation, and the use of the "good cop, bad cop" routine. One prosecutor explained that as long as an investigator avoids doing  or saying anything they would be embarrassed showing a judge or a jury they should have nothing to worry about.

# The Confession

*Developing an admission of guilt into a confession*

Developing the details of the offense from the suspect is sometimes just as difficult and time-consuming as eliciting the first admission of guilt. An efficient means of eliciting the first admission of guilt is by asking an alternative question such as, "Was this the first time you ever did something

---

[44] (Lasiter, Geers, Handley, Weiland and Munhall, *Videotaped Interrogations and Confessions: A Simple Change in Camera Perspective Alters Verdicts in Simulated Trials*, 87 Journal of Applied Psychology 867 (2002). *See, also*, Lassiter, *Illusory Causation in the Courtroom*, 11 Current Directions in Psychological Science 204 (2002).)

[45] An Evaluation;  Research Series, London Home Office Police Dept. 2002.

like this, or have you done things like this your whole life? It was the first time, wasn't it?" Once the suspect has accepted one of the choices provided in the alternative question the investigator should offer the suspect a *statement of reinforcement*, such as "Good, that's what I thought it was all along" or "I was hoping that was the case." It is unrealistic to expect the suspect to launch into a narrative explaining the details of the offense immediately following their first admission of guilt. Therefore the investigator should begin asking brief open-ended questions to develop the details of the offense and avoid asking any leading questions. For example: "What happened next?"; "Then what did you do?"; "How many times did this happen?" The questions should be asked in such a manner so as not to reveal *dependent evidence* that was held back for corroboration purposes – to assess the veracity of the confession. Defense attorneys will be reviewing the tapes carefully to determine whether the investigator intentionally or inadvertently revealed critical elements of the crime to the suspect. Even though a suspect has admitted guilt they will still be reluctant to accept full responsibility for what they have done and therefore attempt to minimize their motive and level of involvement. Investigators have to exercise patience and allow the suspect to relate the details of the offense at their own pace.

When developing the initial details of the crime, the investigator should not ask leading questions. An example of an improper dialogue with leading questions is as follows:

Investigator    (I):    "So you are the person who robbed the clerk in the 7-Eleven®?"

Suspect (S): "Yeah."

I: "And you did this at 9:30 on March 12th of this year?"

S: "Yeah."

I: "During the robbery you stole $237 in cash and cigarettes?"

S: "Yep."

After the suspect has provided a general account of their involvement the investigator should summarize what the suspect said and develop further details as to how the crime was committed and determine the suspect's motive for committing the crime. Following these questions the investigator should try to corroborate the confession.

*Correcting the suspect's choice of the alternative*

If the investigator believes, based on case facts and evidence, that the suspect's choice of the alternative question is not the complete truth, an attempt should be made to obtain a correction from the suspect. For example, a suspect who initially admits they accidentally caused the cigarette burn marks found on their child is trying to minimize their level of responsibility. The location and severity of the burn marks may make it clear that the suspect's admission is not the complete truth. The investigator will need to use a different alternative question to elicit the truth by telling the suspect, "There is no doubt that this was not an accident and that you did this intentionally. What we need to determine is whether you did this because you were angry and frustrated or to maliciously harm her." The suspect's frame of mind at this stage of the interrogation is such that he is likely to answer the investigator's questions as truthfully as he can.

*Maintaining privacy*

While developing the confession it will make it easier for the suspect to relate the details of the crime if he remains in the same room alone with the investigator. At this critical stage of the interrogation the investigator should avoid bringing anyone new into the interrogation room and the suspect should not be moved to another room to record the confession. In addition, the investigator should not take any written notes until the suspect has provided all of the necessary details and corroboration. Since the confession is being electronically recorded the investigator does not have to worry about forgetting various details the suspect may reveal.

*Suspect demonstrations of the criminal behavior*

Having the suspect demonstrate or re-enact various aspects of his crime on videotape can be more powerful than the spoken word. Investigators should ask the suspect to demonstrate various aspects of their criminal actions rather than describe them. For example, in a physical abuse case resulting in the death of a two-year-old child the investigator asked the suspect; "How hard did her head hit the toilet after you pushed her?" The suspect responded, "I don't know, pretty hard." The investigator then asked her to demonstrate, "Why don't you hit the wall there with your hand as hard as her head hit that toilet." The suspect proceeded to hit the wall with her fist and a loud thud could be heard on the tape. Hearing this, the jury could easily imagine the damage an impact of that force would cause to a two-year-old child's head hitting the edge of a ceramic toilet.   In another case a suspect stated "I had my hand on her shirt like this." while confessing to sexually assaulting one of his high school students.   While making this statement the suspect placed his right hand over his heart effectively demonstrating how he touched her breast.   Sometimes actions speak louder than words.

*Establishing the suspect's state of mind*

Establishing the suspect's state of mind at the time the crime was committed  may provide the prosecutor with evidence to counter a defense plea of insanity.   To accomplish this investigators should ask questions to establish the suspects emotional state before, during and after committing the crime. Consider the following dialog from an interview with a mother who sexually abused her 10-year-old son:


I.      "How did you feel prior to sexually assaulting your son?"

S.      "I was looking forward to what I was going to do."

I.      "How did you feel during?"

S.      "I was enjoying what I was doing."

I.      "How did you feel after?"

S.      "I hated myself for what I did."


The suspect clearly established that she knowingly and intentionally sexually abused her son.

Investigators should also ask questions to establish what the suspect was doing before and after they committed the crime such as:

"What were you doing prior to (crime)?"; "What did you do after (crime)?"; "Who did you see or talk to before and after (crime)?" If the suspect did speak to others immediately prior to or following the crime this may lead the investigator to a potential witness to the crime or at the very least someone who can attest to the suspect's demeanor before and after the crime.

*Developing a summary of a suspect's confession*

When a suspect has made a variety of admissions at different times during the interrogation it can be helpful to have the suspect summarize their admissions in a concise statement at the conclusion of the interrogation. This practice avoids the burden of the jury having to listen to several hours of interrogation and piece together the various admissions made by the suspect. The summary statement made by the suspect will help the jury to understand exactly what the suspect is admitting in a complete concise manner. This will also provide the prosecuting attorney the opportunity to use this summary confession to expedite their review of the case and assess its strength.

*Treatment of the suspect by the interrogators*

Even though the judge and jury will be able to make their own assessment regarding the treatment of the suspect by the investigators by listening to or watching the recording of the interrogation, the suspect's own description of how he was treated may influence their perception. Investigators can establish this by asking the suspect a few simple questions following their confession such as: "How do you feel you were treated here today?"; "Did anyone threaten you in any way or promise you anything in exchange for your cooperation?"; "Why did you decide to tell the truth?" The suspect's response to these questions may work to further establish the voluntariness of their confession.   One suspect in an employee theft investigation responded to these questions by stating, "I just feel so much better getting this off my chest.  I will take the penalty, whatever it is. Hopefully it won't be very severe.  I expect to lose my job.  They have every right to take me to court – I did take the money."  Having these statements recorded following the suspect's confession will make it difficult for the defense to argue that this was anything less than a voluntary confession.

*Departments that on their own volition decide to electronically record interview and interrogations*

As stated earlier, there are hundreds of Police Departments who voluntarily electronically record suspect interviews and interrogations.  In such cases it is important that the department establish a written policy regarding the electronic recording of suspect interviews.  Some suggestions with respect to the content of such a policy include: the philosophy of the department regarding electronic recording, the types of crimes where suspects should be recorded, whether it is to be videotape or audio recording, the procedures of electronic recording, maintaining the integrity of the electronic recording, and the conduct of the investigators.  (An example of a department's policy regarding electronic recording can be found in Appendix D.)

# Recommendations

*Miranda General Guidelines*

1. All of the warnings should be given so that the suspect clearly understands what he is being told.

2. If a custodial suspect indicates, at any time, or in any manner whatsoever, that he does not want to talk, the interrogation must cease. The interrogator is not privileged to "talk him out of" his refusal to talk.

3. If a custodial suspect says, at any time, that he wants a lawyer, the interrogation must cease until he has the opportunity to confer with a lawyer, and no further questions may be asked of him outside the lawyer's presence or without the lawyer's permission.

4. If the suspect makes an ambiguous request for an attorney, the investigator should clarify the request by asking, "Do you want an attorney or not?"

5. Under most circumstances the only time a police interrogation may be conducted of a suspect who is in custody or otherwise restrained of his freedom is after he has been given the required warnings and after he has indicated his willingness to answer questions. Once that waiver is given, the interrogator may proceed to interrogate.

---

[46] Unless the investigator can establish this was an emergency rescue or life saving situation. For example, the police are attempting to locate a kidnapped person and are about to interrogate a suspect they have reason to believe knows the location of the victim and time is a critical factor. See Criminal Interrogations and Confessions, p. 515

6. When there is any concern that the suspect's waiver of Miranda rights may be challenged as a result of young age, low IQ, drug or alcohol intoxication, etc., the investigator should ask the suspect what each right means to him.

*Investigator Conduct*

1. Written notes should be taken during the interview even though the interview is being electronically recorded.

2. Questions should be asked in the early stages of the interview to establish the subject's emotional, psychological, and physical well being.

3. A policy should be established whether to obtain consent from the subject to electronically record the interview. State laws (Appendix H) and the prosecuting attorneys preference should be considered.

4. The subject should be continuously recorded while in the interrogation room to include, Miranda, the interview, the interrogation, the confession, and any time the subject was left alone in the room.

5. Any false statements made to a suspect should be intrinsic to the facts of the alleged offense. Investigators should be prepared to explain to the court why the false statement was made.

6. A distinction must be made between false statements (which may be permissible) and manufacturing evidence (which is not permissible).

7. Avoid statements that imply a promise of leniency.

8. Avoid statements that imply a threat to the suspect.

9. Investigators should avoid asking leading questions when corroborating the suspect's confession.

10. The suspect should summarize their admissions in a concise statement at the conclusion of the interrogation.

11. Questions should be asked to establish how the suspect felt he was treated by the investigators.

# Chapter 4

## SPECIAL SITUATIONS

There are special circumstances that investigators encounter which create unique problems concerning the electronic recording of interviews and interrogations, such as child abuse victim interviews; interviewing and interrogating multiple suspects; interviewing a juvenile offender whose parents or guardian are present during the questioning; interviewing a custodial suspect apprehended in the field; or a situation in which multiple investigators are in the interrogation room. In this chapter we will discuss these special situations and how they may affect the electronically recording the interview and interrogation.

## Child Abuse Victims

Although not required by law, there are situations when it would be prudent to electronically record child abuse victim interviews. Even though electronically recording the interview may document some inconsistencies in a victim's statement, the electronically recorded interview can become an essential and sometimes only piece of evidence in the investigation.

Using electronically recorded victim interviews as evidence is not a novel idea. There are at least 39 states that now explicitly authorize at least some use of videotaped interviews of child abuse victims.[47] Scandinavia has been videotaping victim interviews for the past forty years;[48] and Great Britain has permitted videotaped forensic interviews of victims to be admitted into evidence at trial since 1991[49]. Professionals in the field have long advocated the importance of videotaping victim interviews so they can be independently evaluated by other professionals.[50] Electronically recording victim interviews can also assist the prosecuting attorney's assessment of the strength of the case and the victim's statements. This will also give them an opportunity to prepare arguments to deal with any inconsistencies that may occur in the victim's statements. The forensic interview[51] of a child abuse victim is challenging and requires a level of expertise that can only be developed through experience and proper training. The defense will have the electronic recording of the child's interview scrutinized by other professionals to assess the credibility of the child's allegations and whether the interviewer engaged in any suggestive behavior or leading questions that unduly influenced the child's

---

[47] Walker, Nancy McAuliff, Perry & Bradley D. The Use of Videotaped Child Testimony: Public Policy Implications, 7 Notre Dame J. L. Ethics & Pun. Pol'y 387, 392-95 (1993).

[48] Spencer, John R. & Flin, Rhona H. The evidence of children: The Law and The Psychology 166 (1990).

[49] For a discussion of current and former British statutes and practice, see Laura C.H. Hoyzano, Variations on a Theme by Pigot: Special Measures Directions for Child Witnesses, 2000 CRIM. L. REV. 250.

[50] State v. Giles, 772 P.2d 191, 199 (Idaho 1989) (citing expert testimony on videotaped interviews) Lamb, Michael E. et al., Making Children into Competent Witnesses: Reactions to the Amicus Brief in In re Michaels, 1 PSYCHOL. PUB. POL'Y & L. 438, 444-45 (1995).

[51] A forensic interview is conducted with a child to determine whether he or she has been abused and if so, produce evidence that will stand up in court. There is no single forensic interviewing model or method endorsed unanimously by experts in the field. Three widely used approaches are the Child Cognitive interview, the Step-Wise interview, and the Narrative Elaboration. A properly conducted forensic interview is legally sound because it is objective, non-leading, and the interviewer will document the interview.

statements. Therefore, these interviews should be only be conducted by investigators who have specialized training in forensic child interviews.[52] An experienced and properly trained forensic interviewer will develop a more accurate, detailed, and unbiased account of the abuse than would an investigator who lacks the proper training.

Electronically recorded interviews of child abuse victims are often

 videotaped in interview rooms specifically designed for children.

The room has a warm decor and may contain toys, stuffed animals, crayons, coloring books and more comfortable chairs than that of a typical

Photo 4-A

police interrogation room. (Photo 4-A)

When videotaping an interview of a child abuse victim the camera angle should have the entire interview room in view. Unlike an adult, young children may get up and move around the room during the interview which can result in videotaped segments of an empty chair if the camera was to remain in a static position focused on the subject's chair. Investigators should be in full view at all times during the interview to allow others to evaluate whether the investigator did anything that may have had a suggestive influence on the child's allegations. This may be

[52] CornerHouse Interagency Child Abuse Evaluation and Training Center is located in Minneapolis, Minnesota and specializes in child forensic interviews. The mission of CornerHouse is to assess suspected child sexual abuse, to coordinate forensic interview services and to provide training for other professionals. www.cornerhousemn.org

manifested in the investigator's tone of voice or nonverbal behavior when using various props, such as anatomically correct dolls, pictures, diagrams, or artwork that are designed to develop the details of the allegation.

Investigators have to exercise patience and allow the child to relate the details of the offense at their own pace. Young children often lack the appropriate vocabulary or they may feel ashamed and embarrassed to articulate the details of the abuse. Offenders have often convinced the child that somehow they are responsible for the abuse. This may inhibit a child's willingness to disclose the details of the offense. If the investigator is impatient and begins to ask leading or suggestive questions it will give the defense an opportunity to attack the credibility of the child's statement.[53]

Videotaping child abuse victim interviews will save the child from experiencing the stress and anxiety of testifying in open court and allow the child to relate the details of the abuse in a more relaxed environment. This may also result in a more detailed account of the allegation.

Research has shown that interviewing a child in a more relaxed atmosphere will enhance a child's memory.[54] Even so, there still may be inconsistencies in a child's statements. Some children do not have a well-developed sense of time and may be unable to consistently identify the exact day the abuse occurred. At the same time, a child's memory will deteriorate over time more quickly than that of an adult.[55]

---

[53] The New Jersey appellate court found that the videotaped interviews of the child victims of a day care facility in the Kelly Michaels case were so permeated with improper suggestion that accuracy could no longer be unraveled for inaccuracy. State v. Michaels, 642 A.2d 1372, 1379-80 (N.J. 1994).

[54] In a study of seven- to nine-year-olds, children in the "interview group" related more information in free recall, answered specific questions more often, and denied information or failed to respond to questions less often than did members of the "courtroom group." Hill, P.E. & Hill, S. M., Videotaping Children's Testimony: An Empirical View, 85 Mich. L. Rev. 809, 815-16 (1987).

[55] Flin, R. et al., The Effect of a Five-Month Delay on Children's and Adults' Eyewitness Memory, 83 Brit. 1. Psychol. 323,333 (1992).

In some cases, because the child abuse victim may be reluctant to relate the details of the abuse and may even deny any abuse in the initial interview, investigators may need to interview the child a second time when the child is more willing to discuss the allegations. While the investigators may be concerned that the initial videotaped interview of the child will provide the defense with evidence to attack the credibility of the child's subsequent allegations, they should electronically record all of the interviews conducted with the victim regardless of the inconsistencies that may develop, and they should certainly refrain from destroying any electronically recorded interviews.[56]

# Multiple Interrogators

In most circumstances we recommend that only one investigator be in the room with the suspect when conducting an interview or interrogation. When a second investigator is in the interrogation room his presence can adversely affect the integrity of the private environment that is oftentimes essential to the effort to elicit truthful information from the suspect. If a second investigator is going to participate in the interview or interrogation, their participation should be carefully orchestrated with the lead investigator. The lead investigator should sit directly across from the

---

[56] In Morgan v. Gertz 166 F.3d 1307 Colorado (10th Cir. 1999) the trial court granted a motion for a directed verdict of acquittal because investigators taped over and therefore virtually destroyed an initial interview where the child "gave no indication she had been the victim of sexual abuse " by her stepfather. This interview was taped over by a subsequent interview six months later where the child alleged that she had been sexually abused by her stepfather. In Memphis, Tennessee day-care investigators videotaped several interviews with child victims of abuse and found a number of inconsistencies in the children's statements. After reviewing the tapes an assistant attorney instructed the investigators to destroy the tapes so that they would not be available for discovery. The Tennessee Supreme Court held that such behavior constituted willful prosecutorial misconduct in violation of Brady v. Maryland 373 U.S. 83 (1963).

suspect while the other investigator sits off to the side, preferably out of direct eyesight of the suspect. Both investigators need to be aware of the camera placement so they do not block the view of the suspect by sitting in front of the camera.

Investigators should decide ahead of time who will conduct the interview and refrain from simultaneously asking questions of the suspect. Simultaneous questioning by two investigators may overwhelm the suspect who may respond by mentally withdrawing from the process. This may also give the appearance to a jury that the investigators were "ganging up" on the suspect. Consequently, during an interrogation one investigator should be a silent observer while the other communicates with the suspect. Investigators should develop a procedure by which a smooth transition can be made during the interview and the interrogation if they decide to change roles from communicator to observer. During the interview, as one investigator completes his questioning, he should simply ask the observer if he has any questions to ask the suspect. If the second investigator does have further questions, it is important that the second investigator switch chairs with the first investigator. The investigator who is asking questions should sit directly in front of the suspect and not question the suspect from across a table.

During the interrogation, investigators should exercise discretion as to how one interrupts the other. If the observer recognizes that his partner is not making any progress he should make a statement to indicate to his partner that he is now taking over, such as, "Mike, what investigator Jayne says is right. We have a lot of information that clearly shows your involvement in this and we both feel it's important that you have an opportunity to explain yourself." This statement should make the transition clear to the other investigator that he should get out of his chair and let the other investigator take over. The original interrogator can then either leave the room under the pretense of checking information or sit in the observer's chair.

Each investigator should remain seated throughout both the interview and the interrogation and should avoid pacing around the room or standing over the suspect. When videotaping interrogations, judges and juries will not only assess what investigators say to a suspect but also their nonverbal behavior. If they see one of the investigators standing over or behind the suspect it may appear threatening.[57]

If the camera angle is such that both investigators are in the frame, as illustrated in Photo 4-B, the investigator who is observing must remember that those watching the videotape will be evaluating each person

Photo 4-B

on the tape. Therefore, the investigator should appear interested and involved in what the other investigator is saying. This can become a challenge if the interrogation is lengthy and the investigator's statements are very familiar to the observer.

Generally we recommend that

---

[57] State of TN v. William A. Payne, Jr. No. E2002-01307-SC-R11-CD  In this case the judge specifically pointed out in his opinion one of the reasons he thought a non-custodial interview became custodial was because "the demeanor, tone, and questioning markedly changed, as did the officer's physical location in the room."  He observed that one officer was partially blocking the suspect's path to the door and the other officer was standing over the suspect.  At this point he ruled the non-custodial interview became custodial and found the suspect's subsequent incriminating statements inadmissible.

investigators avoid using the **"good guy / bad guy routine."** Although this has been accepted by the courts,[58] this approach may create the impression with the jury that the investigators were acting in a threatening manner and could contribute to a finding that the confession was involuntary. The *good guy / bad guy routine* also plays into the stereotyped portrayal of police interrogations as seen on television and may be viewed by the suspect as a transparent police tactic designed to manipulate him into confessing. This may damage the credibility of the investigators and make it more difficult to elicit the truth from the suspect.

To reiterate, in most cases we have found that having a single investigator conduct an interrogation is preferable to two investigators. If two investigators are going to participate in the interrogation, they should work as a team and reinforce what the other is saying, as opposed to one investigator assuming an adversarial role in the interrogation. Finally, only one investigator at a time should be communicating with the suspect.

# Multiple Suspect Interrogations

Due to the expense involved in equipping interrogation rooms to electronically record custodial interviews and interrogations, some departments may only have one interrogation room equipped for electronic recording. This can create a problem when investigators have multiple suspects to question about their involvement in the same crime. Investigators can either interview suspects one at a time in the interrogation room equipped for recording or interview suspects simultaneously and not record one or more of the interviews.

---

[58] Foth v. State, 1990 WL 152703, (Minn. Ct. App. Oct. 16, 1990) (No. C6-90-473) found that the defendant had not been coerced into making a statement by the "good cop/bad cop" police interrogation tactic.

Even though some statutory regulations[59] identify this type of situation as an exemption to the requirement of electronically recording, this can be problematic when the suspects who were not electronically recorded make incriminating statements. The defense may use this as an opportunity to suggest that the investigator engaged in improper interrogation tactics with the suspects who were not electronically recorded. This argument may appear especially credible if the suspect who was recorded did not make any incriminating statements.

Investigators could avoid this situation by simply having portable electronic recording equipment available for use in any interview room or office. Even if only an audio recording of the interviews and interrogations is made, it would document what was said along with any incriminating statements that were made by the suspect.

Most investigators find it advantageous to interview and interrogate multiple suspects simultaneously in separate rooms because it provides them an opportunity to employ interrogation tactics specifically designed for these situations. For example, one interrogation technique often employed with multiple suspects is to play one suspect against the other. In this approach the investigator will inform the suspect, "We are going to believe whoever talks first" and by saying nothing it will appear that the suspect is principally responsible. The investigator may even intimate to

---

[59] Illinois statute 18 provides that, in homicide cases, statements made as a result of custodial interrogation in a place of detention are presumptively inadmissible if not electronically recorded. An exception to this rule is when multiple suspects are being questioned and all available recording equipment is being utilized for other suspects.

[60] The U.S. Supreme court ruled in Frazier v. Cupp, 394 U.S. 731, 89 S. Ct. 1420 (1969) that lying to a suspect about his partner confessing will not, in itself, invalidate the voluntariness of a suspect's confession when taking into consideration the "totality of the circumstances."

one suspect that his accomplice has already confessed and point out the futility of his continued denials.[60]

# Juvenile Interrogations

In those situations in which a parent or legal guardian is going to be in the interrogation room during the questioning of a juvenile, the investigators should first seek the cooperation and understanding of the juvenile's parents or guardian. When dealing with parents who are overly protective of their child or are naive about their child's behavior, it is important that the investigator explain to them, outside of the child's presence, general investigative findings and the nature of the questioning process that is about to take place. The goal is to avoid electronically recording any arguments or objections the parent (guardian) may voice during the interview.

The parent (guardian) should be advised that a non-accusatory *interview* of their child will be conducted to determine whether he has any knowledge of or involvement in the offense that is under investigation. The parents should be further advised that if in the investigator's opinion their child is not involved in the crime, the child will be released. On the other hand, if the investigator believes that the child is involved, the matter should be discussed with the parents, emphasizing the need to correct the problem before it becomes more serious. The investigator should ask the parents (guardian) for their cooperation in this process and instruct them to observe and listen while they are in the interview room, but not to interrupt the questioning.

Prior to the *interrogation* the parents should be advised that the results of the investigation show that their child is involved in the offense under investigation. To encourage the parent's cooperation it can be effective for the investigator to make a statement similar to the following:

> *"No one is blaming you for your child's involvement in this crime. This does not mean that you have been negligent in bringing up (child) or that you are bad parents. There are times in every child's life when peer pressure is stronger than parental pressure and every child makes mistakes. All kids do things wrong. It doesn't mean that they are going to be career criminals but it is important that the child learn from his mistake so something like this doesn't happen again."*

The investigator should then explain to the parents (guardian) the nature of the interrogation themes that will be developed and that their child will probably attempt to deny any involvement.[61]

# Out-of-Office Interviews

*The use of portable electronic recording equipment*

Even though most statutory regulations specify that the electronic recording of a custodial interview and interrogation is required when conducted in a *place of detention* or when *feasible*, investigators will inevitably run into situations where they may have to question a custodial suspect in the field. For example, when an officer apprehends a suspect who was seen running out of a liquor store wearing a mask and holding a gun, and who has been identified as the robber by the liquor store clerk, it

---

[61] For a complete explanation of theme development of juvenile suspects see <u>Criminal Interrogations and Confessions</u>, by Inbau, Reid, Buckley, Jayne 2001, pgs. 298-303.

may be very advantageous for the officer to immediately question the suspect (after the appropriate advisement of rights and subsequent waiver) while they are sitting in his squad car as opposed to waiting until they get back to the station. If the suspect makes any incriminating statements at this time and the officer is not equipped to electronically record those statements, the defense may argue that the statements should be suppressed. In an effort to avoid this challenge, departments should equip investigators with mobile video recording equipment or audio pocket recorders.[62] If investigators are not equipped with portable recording devices any incriminating statements made by a custodial suspect outside of a place of detention may be suppressed.[63]

When using portable pocket recorders, investigators should be careful to place the recorder in a location where rustling of clothing will not interfere with the recording quality. An external microphone that can be attached to the investigator's shirt should be used to avoid this problem. To avoid the recording of any embarrassing or inappropriate comments by other investigators it should be made clear to fellow investigators, "We're going on tape" so they are aware that everything they say from that point forward will be on the record.

Most **analog** pocket recorders allow the operator to adjust the

---

[62] Minnesota statutory regulations consider a *place of detention* to include MPD vehicles equipped with Mobile Video Recording (MVR) equipment and therefore investigators are required to electronically record all interrogations conducted in such a vehicle to include any information about rights, any waiver of those rights, and all questioning. A reprint of a portion of the MPD policy on MVR can be found in Appendix E.

[63] Recording interviews State v. Scales by Assistant Attorney General James P. Spencer *"Avoiding issuing officers tape recorders to avert the recording requirement will certainly be viewed as a policy that will result in suppression of the statement, regardless of the arresting officer's good faith. Therefore, we recommend that any peace officer who may question suspects in squads be issued recorders or video-cameras."*

recording speed to increase the recording time of the tape. If this is set to the longest recording time this may have a negative impact on the quality of the recording. Therefore, the pocket recorders should be set to normal recording speed. In addition, the investigator needs to be aware of the time

so that the tape can be changed in the recorder before it runs out. Investigators can avoid this problem by using digital recorders.

Digital recorders use a memory card instead of analog tape. A 128MB memory card will allow up to 45 hours of recording and the digital format is easily downloaded to a computer, making storage convenient and the files accessible to other investigators. The interviews can be e-mailed to other investigators for review or to support staff for transcription.

*Malfunction of portable equipment*

If an investigator's portable electronic recording equipment fails (i.e. batteries are dead, the tape is broken, the investigator runs out of tape, or the stop button is inadvertently pressed), he should be prepared to offer a reasonable explanation for the malfunction at trial. If the investigator ran out of tape or the batteries went dead, he will need to use his best judgment as to whether it would have been *feasible* to continue recording the interview or interrogation. If the investigator is in a situation where he could immediately have purchased new batteries or a tape at a nearby store, the courts may not accept the argument that it was not feasible to continue recording. However, if the investigator can make a reasonable explanation why he was unable to remedy the situation he should continue with the interview. Common sense dictates that investigators should be equipped with spare batteries and tapes to handle these situations or to be prepared to explain why they were not prepared for these contingencies.

In situations where a custodial suspect's statements made outside of an interview room are not electronically recorded, the investigator should immediately do so upon returning to the station house. In addition to electronically recording the suspect's statements, the investigator should document the reason why the suspect's statements were not electronically recorded earlier. e.g., equipment malfunction; the tape ran out; it was an "emergency situation"– for example someone's life was in danger and the suspect had critical information concerning their whereabouts.

*Domestic violence investigations*

When investigating domestic violence, investigators should activate their pocket recorders prior to entering the home. In some cases this will give the investigator an opportunity to record the disturbance (crying, yelling, or fighting) as they approach the residence. This extemporaneous recording may provide a judge or jury with a firsthand account of the situation. The investigators should then separate the parties and record their statements individually.

# Recommendations

1. Child victims of abuse should be interviewed in a room specifically designed for children.

2. The camera angle in child victim interviews should be "equal focus" showing the child and the interviewer at all times.

3. When two investigators are present during an interview, only one investigator at a time should be communicating with the suspect.

4. Investigators should develop a procedure by which a smooth transition can be made during the interview or interrogation if they decide to change roles from communicator to observer.

5. Avoid using the "good guy / bad guy routine."

6. When interviewing multiple suspects simultaneously where only one interrogation room is equipped to record, an audio recording of each interview should be made using portable pocket digital recorders.

7. Out-of-office suspect interviews should be recorded using digital pocket recorders.

8. When recording out-of-office, advise fellow investigators "We are going on tape," to avoid recording any embarrassing or inappropriate comments by other investigators.

9. When interviewing juveniles, seek parental (guardian) understanding and cooperation prior to recording and outside of the child's presence.

# Chapter 5

## OFFERING TESTIMONY IN ELECTRONICALLY RECORDED INTERROGATIONS

In previous chapters the benefits of electronically recording interviews and interrogations have been emphasized. However, during our interviews with prosecuting attorneys, the most common drawback mentioned was the investigator's testimony in cases where the interrogation was electronically recorded. The problems ranged from the investigator not being able to adequately explain why certain things were done or said, to possibly misleading testimony that appeared to support defense claims of coercion or compulsion.

Interviewing and interrogation are complex procedures that require specific training as well as a fair amount of experience to master. During this training there are underlying psychological and legal issues covered, but it is the actual application of the techniques and procedures that are reinforced with successful field experience. As a consequence, an investigator can be very competent in conducting interviews and interrogations, but may not be able to accurately describe underlying principles to a judge or jury. For example, when a videotape shows the investigator moving closer to a suspect during an interrogation, he knows that it is proper to encroach on the suspect's space but may not be able to recall the psychological basis for the procedure. Under this circumstance, the defense attorney may even persuade the investigator to offer inaccurate testimony where the witness agrees that the reason he moved closer to the suspect was to exert authority and control over the person, thereby implying coercion.

There is no question that an electronically recorded interrogation places the investigator's conduct under increased scrutiny during a trial. The defense can pick apart particular words or actions and offer a distorted perception of the actual interrogation. In one trial a psychologist, after viewing a videotaped interrogation formed an opinion that the investigator had inadvertently hypnotized the defendant. Specifically, the psychologist testified that, "The investigator presented a monologue in a hypnotic pattern. His (the interrogator's) voice was slow and soothing and he kept repeating the same concept." Based on the psychologist's testimony, the judge suppressed the defendant's murder confession.[64]

Unfortunately, movie and television portrayals of police interrogation prepare a judge and jury to expect aggressive and threatening behavior by the interrogator. At one time this may have been typical interrogation conduct. Over the years, however, police interrogation techniques have become much more psychologically sophisticated. Substantial efforts have been made to understand the guilty suspect's thought process during the commission of a crime as well as during the interrogation.[65] This body of knowledge has been used to develop more

---

[64] People v. DeLisle, 183 Mich app. 713, 455 N.W. 2d 401 (1990).

[65] During the early development of the Reid Technique, Fred Inbau interviewed death-row inmates in an effort to find out what statements or techniques the interrogator used that were effective in persuading the person to tell the truth. Reid and Associates has continued this effort through similar interviews with gang members, rapists and child molesters.

effective techniques of persuading a suspect to tell the truth. The foundation for the various seminars and courses that teach interviewing and interrogation to law enforcement investigators is the Reid Technique. Consequently, we will start with an overview of the principles developed in this internationally recognized approach to interviewing and interrogating criminal suspects.

# Overview of the Reid Technique[66]

The Reid technique defines a three-step approach to an investigation. The first step is referred to as **factual analysis**, which simply represents the collection and analysis of information surrounding a crime as well as possible suspects. This information can come from physical evidence collected at a crime scene, victim, witness or informant statements, personal observations, record or background checks. A primary goal of factual analysis is to develop a list of possible suspects and to rank order each suspect's probable involvement in the crime based on opportunity, access, motive, propensity and evidence. A second important goal is to identify information that can be used to corroborate a confession, if one is obtained in the investigation.

*Dependent corroboration* is defined as information purposely withheld from the suspect and the media. The lead investigator should document, in the case file, what information about the crime will be preserved for dependent corroboration. This information should be distinct

---

[66] For a complete and in-depth presentation of the Reid Technique, see Inbau, F., Reid, J., Buckley, J., & Jayne, B. Criminal Interrogation and Confessions 4th ed. Aspen Publications, Maryland 2001.

enough where the guilty person would certainly remember it, but not so critical as to impair the ability to conduct a proper interview. Examples of dependent corroboration include the direction in which a get-away car left the scene of a robbery, an unusual statement made to a rape or robbery victim or the method of entering a home that was burglarized. The fact that a suspect can provide dependent corroboration about the crime strongly supports the trustworthiness of his confession.

Unfortunately, there have been occasions where investigators have inadvertently revealed dependent corroboration to a suspect, thus possibly tainting a confession. For this reason, the investigator should always attempt to obtain *independent corroboration* during a confession. This is defined as information not known until the confession, and which is independently verified following the confession. Examples of independent corroboration include the present location of a murder weapon or fruits of a crime, to whom the suspect sold stolen property or where he had a key duplicated.

The second step of the Reid Technique is **the interview**. The Reid Technique makes a very clear distinction between interviewing and interrogation. Furthermore, it is our strong recommendation not to combine the two procedures, for they both have unique and separate purposes and procedures. The following are characteristics of an interview:

*The interview is non-accusatory.* This is so even when the investigator has strong reason to believe the suspect is involved in the offense. Even when the investigator knows that the suspect has lied to a question, the investigator's demeanor is still non-accusatory.[67] The reason

---

[67] An exception to this rule is when a suspect exhibits a clear desire to confess during the interview. Under this circumstance, it would be appropriate for the investigator to encourage the suspect to tell the truth, which may involve an accusatory statement or tone.

for this is that once an investigator becomes accusatory, the suspect becomes guarded and will not volunteer information. Furthermore, if the suspect has been previously advised of his right to remain silent and right to an attorney, an accusatory tone by the investigator puts the suspect on the defensive, thereby encouraging the suspect to invoke his constitutional rights.

*The interview consists of a question-and-answer format.* **During the first few minutes of the interview, the investigator should ask** non-threatening background questions, perhaps inquiring about the suspect's living situation, employment, school, or general well-being. The purpose for these questions is to establish baseline information about the suspect, e.g., intelligence, communication skills, normal level of eye contact, general nervous tension, etc. The remaining questions asked during the interview address the crime under investigation. In this regard, the Reid technique teaches that during an interview the proportion of talking should be 20% for the investigator and 80% for the suspect. To maintain this balance, the investigator should try to ask questions that require a narrative response, keep questions short and avoid rambling or offering too much information to the suspect.

*The purpose for conducting an interview is to elicit information.* In some cases the investigator may have such incriminating evidence against a suspect that when this evidence is presented during the interview, a full confession is immediately forthcoming. Absent overwhelming evidence, however, most suspects will deny involvement in a crime. There are three broad categories of information an investigator wants to elicit during an interview. The first is termed **investigative information**. These questions address the suspect's opportunity, access and motives as well as an explanation for any evidence that has surfaced. The second category of information elicited during the interview relates specifically to **establishing the suspect's probable guilt or innocence**. The most accurate means to assess the suspect's credibility, other than through the polygraph technique, is by asking *behavior-provoking* questions during the interview. Research has demonstrated that these questions tend to be answered differently by suspects who are verified as innocent of a crime compared to suspects who are verified as guilty of a crime.[68] The final category of information developed during an interview is used to **profile the suspect for an interrogation**. Examples of this information includes the type of consequence (real or personal) the suspects is most concerned about, the flexibility of the consequence, underlying defense mechanisms the suspect is utilizing to justify the crime, and identifying whether the suspect is concerned that certain evidence (fingerprints, DNA, surveillance video, etc.) may implicate him in the crime. This insight is used to develop an interrogation strategy for the suspect.

Finally, during an interview designed to assess a suspect's credibility, *the investigator should take active written notes*. By active note-taking, we mean literally that following each response to an interview question, the investigator writes out the essence of the suspect's response. The primary benefit of active note-taking is that it slows down the pace of questioning. It is much easier to lie to a series of questions that are asked rapidly than questions which are separated by five to seven seconds of

---

[68] Horvath, F., Jayne, B. & Buckley, J. "Differentiation of Truthful and Deceptive Criminal Suspects in Behavior Analysis Interviews," Forensic Journal of Science 39, 3. 793-806, 1994.

silence. The silence created by active note-taking elevates the deceptive suspect's fear of detection and enhances the investigator's ability to detect deception. Also, by slowing down the pace of questioning, the investigator is afforded more time to observe and analyze the suspect's behavior and to formulate appropriate follow-up questions. Conversely, a rapid-fire questioning approach may cause an innocent suspect to appear deceptive in their posture and eye contact and even to offer inconsistent responses as a result of confusion. In summary, even though the interview is being videotaped, for the above reasons, it is our recommendation that the investigator create silence between each interview question by writing out the essence of the suspect's response.

The final stage of the Reid Technique is **the interrogation** which occurs when the investigator has formed a reasonable belief that the suspect is guilty of the crime. This belief may be based on behavioral observations during the interview, circumstantial, testimonial or physical evidence. If possible, we advocate that the interview and interrogation be separated by a period of perhaps ten minutes. This procedure allows the investigator time alone to develop an interrogation strategy and also clearly separates the non-accusatory interview from the accusatory interrogation.

*The interrogation is accusatory but the investigator's demeanor is understanding.* If an investigator is going to be successful at persuading a suspect to tell the truth about his involvement in a crime, the investigator must express high confidence in the suspect's guilt. Consequently, the interrogation is based on a presumption of guilt, which is accusatory. On the other hand, the investigator does not want the suspect to feel threatened, which will invoke a fight-or-flight response. The investigator, therefore, assumes a demeanor that expresses high confidence in the suspect's guilt, but also one that is understanding toward the suspect's decision to commit the crime. The goal here is not to frighten the suspect out of confessing but rather to create an environment where the suspect feels comfortable telling the truth.

*The interrogation represents a monologue.* One of the significant revelations from post-confession interviews of criminal suspects is that a person who is guilty of committing a crime has justified that crime in some manner. It does not matter what crime the suspect committed – theft, arson, rape, fraud, assault or murder, in the guilty suspect's mind he believed that his crime was somewhat justified. During an interrogation the investigator reinforces the suspect's own justification for the crime. These justifications and excuses are presented as a monologue where the suspect is encouraged to listen to the investigator.

On the other hand it is psychologically wrong to ask accusatory questions during an interrogation such as, "I don't believe you. Tell me again where you were last Friday!" "You killed her, didn't you!" Accusatory questions of this nature simply encourage denials from the suspect. To ease the task of the suspect deciding to tell the truth during an interrogation, an investigator should not ask the suspect questions about his involvement in the crime until he is ready to make the first admission of guilt.

*The purpose for conducting an interrogation is to elicit the truth.*

The majority of interrogations are conducted on suspects who are guilty of the crime and their subsequent confession represents the truth. However, any investigator who conducts interrogations on a regular basis will eventually interrogate a suspect who is innocent of the crime under investigation. Some of these suspects will have lied about their alibi or have withheld guilty knowledge about a crime. In other cases, the suspect is innocent of any wrongdoing but may simply be caught in a web of circumstantial evidence. If the interrogation reveals the false alibi, guilty knowledge or otherwise establishes the suspect's innocence, it is a successful interrogation because the truth was learned.

*The interrogation relies extensively on pretense and duplicity.* In those extremely rare cases where the investigator has overwhelming evidence indicating the suspect's involvement in a crime, the interrogation represents a factual presentation of the evidence which will almost always result in a forthcoming confession.[69] In the majority of investigations, there is no prima facie evidence proving the suspect's guilt, which is precisely why the interrogation is being conducted – in an effort to obtain such evidence. For an investigator to successfully persuade a suspect to tell the truth, a number of deceptive tactics are often required, including overstating confidence in the suspect's guilt, establishing a false pretense for the interrogation, offering the suspect disingenuous compliments or flatter and even lying outright about being in possession of incriminating evidence.

---

[69] In most situations the investigator only has weak evidence suggesting the suspect's probable guilt. Under this circumstance the investigator should not present this evidence since it tends to strengthen the guilty suspect's resolve to continue denying involvement in the offense once he realizes that the police do not have a strong case against him.

# The Reid Nine Steps of Interrogation

The interrogation approach taught in the Reid Technique is referred to as the Reid Nine Steps of Interrogation. The interrogation is broken down into steps or stages not only to help learn the material, but because suspects go through various steps or stages in their decision to tell the truth. The following is an overview of the nine steps.

Step One is the **direct positive confrontation**. The interrogation begins with the investigator directly accusing the suspect of involvement in the offense. An example confrontation statement would be as follows, "Rick, I have in this folder the results of our entire investigation and based on all of the evidence we have collected, there is no doubt that you (committed crime)." At this point the investigator would sit down approximately $3^1/_2$ feet directly in front of the suspect and make a statement such as, "Rick, I want to sit down with you this afternoon to get this thing clarified."

Step Two is **theme development**. An interrogation theme is a monologue presented by the investigator during which reasons and excuses are offered to psychologically and morally justify the suspect's crime. These excuses may place blame away from the suspect, minimize the moral seriousness of the crime or re-describe the intention behind some aspect of the suspect's crime. In essence, the excuse allows the suspect to save face. The Reid Technique clearly teaches that an investigator should not suggest a theme that would remove criminal responsibility from the suspect.

Steps Three and Four relate to **handling the suspect's denials and**

**overcoming objections**. At this stage of the interrogation the investigator has told the suspect that the evidence clearly indicates his guilt and that the reason the investigator is talking to the suspect further is because he or she believes that there may be circumstances that led to the suspect's decision to commit the crime (the interrogation theme). Because the investigator has not produced any evidence of the suspect's guilt, the suspect is likely to test the investigator's confidence by denying involvement in the offense. The goal of the investigator is to discourage denials from surfacing, for the more often the suspect denies involvement in the crime, the more difficult it is for the suspect to tell the truth. If the suspect's denials are ineffective in decreasing the investigator's confidence, the suspect may offer an objection. An objection is a reason or excuse as to why the suspect would not commit the crime, e.g., "I wasn't raised to do things like that"; "I wouldn't risk going back to jail!" The investigator rewards the objection and incorporates it within the theme, e.g., "I'm glad you mentioned that because it tells me this was out of character for you."

During almost every interrogation, the suspect enters a stage where his thoughts turn inward and are focused on consequences the suspect now faces. Psychologically, the suspect withdraws and is very content to sit in the chair and wait out the investigator. During Step Five, the investigator must **procure the suspect's attention**. This can be done by physically moving closer to the suspect, asking hypothetical questions and attempting to catch the suspect's eye contact by directing the theme to the suspect's eyes.

At some point, hopefully, the suspect begins to consider telling the truth. There are fairly reliable nonverbal signs that indicate the suspect is in Step Six, **the passive mood**. At this stage the suspect often will uncross his arms and legs and his eyes will drop to the floor. His posture may collapse as he leans forward in the chair, bowing his head in a submissive manner. A tear may roll down the suspect's cheek. These behaviors indicate that the investigator should discontinue theme development and attempt to elicit the first admission of guilt by asking an alternative question.

Step Seven is the **presentation of an alternative question**. An alternative question offers the suspect two choices concerning some aspect of this crime, accepting either choice represents the first admission of guilt. Examples of alternative questions include, "Have you been doing things like this your whole life or was this just the first time?"; "Was this whole thing your idea or did you get talked into it?"; "Did you take that money and blow it on parties and drugs or was it needed to help out your family?" To encourage the suspect to make the first admission of guilt, the investigator eventually asks one side of the alternative question in a leading manner, e.g., "You took it to help out your family, didn't you?"

If the suspect acknowledges the alternative question the interrogation moves to Step Eight, **developing the oral confession**. This is accomplished by first committing the suspect to his initial admission by asking questions about the crime that require brief answers. Eventually, the investigator's questions become more in-depth in an effort to learn the full details of the crime, along with information that can be used to corroborate the confession. Step Nine is **converting the confession to a court-admissible document**. This may involve the suspect writing out his own confession, the suspect signing a confession written by the investigator or having the confession electronically recorded (see Chapter 2).

The following recommendations for offering testimony come from our staff's many years of experience testifying on expert opinions as well as confessions. Additional insight was offered from the interviews with the Minnesota prosecutors. The reader should recognize that the following responses are merely suggestions. Certainly, the investigator must answer all questions truthfully when testifying. Because of the electronic recording, the court will already know what was done and said during the interview and interrogation. Consequently, much of the investigator's testimony will address explanations for his conduct, e.g., "Why didn't you let the suspect talk?", "Weren't you forcing the defendant to confess by only giving him two choices concerning the crime?" In this regard, it will be the investigator's responsibility to accurately educate the court about interviewing and interrogation procedures.

# Guidelines When Offering Testimony

*Sit up straight and do not hide your hands.*

Much of the investigator's credibility in court is based on observing nonverbal behavior. The witness should assume an open and comfortable posture, maintain appropriate eye contact, and keep his hands out of contact with his body and visible.

*Speak clearly and address your answer to the attorney who asked the question.*

The witness should avoid the unconscious temptation of looking toward their own attorney for assistance.

*Delay each response by a period of about two seconds.*

Establishing a pattern of a short pause before answering questions allows the witness a little time to formulate each response. In addition, it provides time for an attorney to object to the question.

*If a question is not clear ask for clarification.*

If the witness asks for too many questions to be clarified he may come across as lacking confidence and using stalling tactics to avoid answering difficult questions. On the other hand, attorneys often ask convoluted questions, compound questions that address two behaviors, or make false assumptions within the question. Under these circumstances it is clearly advisable for the witness to ask for a portion of the question to be clarified, request an example of what the attorney is referring to or correct a false assumption included in the question.

*Do not volunteer more information than what was asked.*

The witness should limit his answer to the information requested in the attorney's question.  On the other hand, if the witness anticipates what the attorney needs to know and volunteers additional information, there is a risk of "opening legal doors" that should remain shut.

*Do not cite case law.*

While it is appropriate to reference legal guidelines or principles, the witness should not offer interpretations of legal decisions unless he is testifying as an expert witness in legal aspects.  For example, if the witness is asked why he did not advise the defendant of Miranda warnings, it would be appropriate to response, "Because he was not in custody at the time I questioned him."  It would be improper to respond, "The 1966 Miranda decision clearly indicates that the required rights need not be administered to someone who is not in custody."

*Avoid arguing with opposing counsel.*

The defense attorney has every right to reasonably challenge a witness' recall, perceptions, or stated intentions.  This is part of providing a competent defense and the witness should not respond emotionally to such challenges.

# Preparing for Testimony

*Review all of the video- or audiotape prior to trial.*

Prior to testifying the investigator should review all of the recorded interview, interrogation and confession, as well as any reports filed in the case. The defense attorney certainly will have spent considerable time identifying areas of the interview or interrogation to attack. The investigator must be familiar enough with the recording to identify whether a particular statement was misquoted or taken out of context.

*Be open with the prosecutor about your concerns.*

After reviewing an interview and interrogation, the investigator may identify certain statements or occurrences that may weaken the prosecution's case. It may be the suspect's ambiguous comment about needing an attorney, the investigator's comment that he wants to "help the suspect out" or perhaps the investigator positioning his chair between the suspect and the door in a non-custodial interrogation. There should be no assumption that the prosecutor's silence is an indication that there are no problems with the interview or interrogation. Because the prosecutor is involved with other matters when preparing a case, often the first indication that there were problems with an interview or interrogation surface as a defense motion to suppress evidence or during the cross-examination of the investigator.

*Discuss with the prosecutor what portions of the interview or confession are not admissible.*

Generally, prior to a trial, the prosecution and defense will stipulate what portions of the electronic recording will be admissible as evidence. As an example, it can be a very meaningful behavior-provoking question to ask a suspect whether or not he would be willing to take a polygraph examination and to predict the results of the examination. However, many states hold that it is a reversible error for an investigator to testify that the defendant refused to take a polygraph examination. The investigator must be careful not to jeopardize the government's case by revealing inadmissible information.

*Should the investigator attempt to qualify as an expert witness?*

An expert witness is a person who, through education, experience or research, has obtained knowledge in a particular field beyond that of a layperson. If an experienced investigator has attended a number of seminars on the topic of interviewing and interrogation and perhaps conducted in-house training or published a number of relevant articles, a judge may qualify the investigator as an expert witness. In addition to enhanced credibility on the witness stand, an expert witness is also permitted to form conclusions within their area of expertise. While this privilege may assist in some areas of testimony, it can also be used against the witness. As an example, the defense attorney may ask the investigator to comment on the significance of every gesture and posture change or verb choice by the suspect during the interview.

*Should the investigator offer testimony concerning the defendant's credibility based on specific behaviors occurring during the interview?*

Unless the investigator is extremely familiar with the research conducted on behavior symptom analysis and is comfortable discussing statistics, research methodology and the underlying psychological principles involved in behavior analysis, it is not advisable to offer opinions of truth or deception based on specific behaviors. A response that falls short of rendering a specific opinion would be something like, "Based on my (12 years) of experience in interviewing both truthful and deceptive suspects, I have found that a frozen and rigid posture during the course of an interview is more typical of a person who is not telling the truth."

*Should the investigator testify that he used the Reid Technique?*

Unless the investigator clearly followed all aspects of the Reid Techniques described during our training seminar and in our textbook, it is our recommendation that the investigator should not testify that he or she used the Reid Technique. To do so may open the investigator to unwarranted attacks during cross examination. A suggested response is for the investigator to testify that he incorporated elements of the Reid Technique within the interrogation.

# Questions Concerning Miranda Issues

*Did you invite the defendant to the police station under a false pretense?*

In some agencies it is a fairly common practice to entice a suspect to voluntarily appear at the station under a false pretense. For example, explaining that a vehicle matching the description of one owned by the suspect was involved in a hit-and-run accident. If a ruse of this nature was used, certainly the investigator should truthfully acknowledge that. This, of course, will lead to a question as to why a false pretense was used, and whether the interview/interrogation session truly was voluntary. One possible explanation for this is that the police did not have probable cause to arrest the suspect and were worried about evidence being destroyed or the suspect leaving the jurisdiction. Some courts have accepted this practice, provided that the suspect was immediately told the truth about the actual purpose for the interview.

*At what point were you convinced that the defendant was guilty?*

While the issue of the investigator's perceptions of the suspect's guilt is generally considered insignificant in determining the necessity of issuing Miranda warnings, a defense attorney may attempt to plant the seed of "perceptual custody" in a judge's mind. This may then be used to argue that Miranda warnings ought to have been given in a non-custodial setting. A satisfactory response to a question relating to the investigator's definite knowledge of the suspect's guilt should make reference to the confession. In other words, an investigator may have had strong suspicions of a suspect's involvement in a crime at the outset of an interrogation, but it was not until the suspect offered a corroborated confession that the investigator knew for certain that the defendant committed the crime.

*Why didn't you give the defendant Miranda warnings earlier?*

To satisfy the legal requirements, the investigator must be able to convince the court that the warnings were not given earlier because the suspect was not in custody earlier. In this regard, it will be important for the witness to establish how the suspect knew that he was not in custody, e.g., the investigator verbally advised the suspect of this, leaving the suspect alone in the room with an unlocked door.

*How do you know the defendant understood the Miranda warnings?*

The investigator may comment on the fact that the suspect was clearly conversant in English and also, if appropriate, that the suspect verbally stated that he understood his rights. If the suspect is young or has a lower intelligence, it is recommended that the investigator specifically ask the suspect what each constitutional right means to him. As an example, the investigator might say, "You have the right to remain silent. What does that mean to you?" The suspect's answers to those types of questions offer the judge the best possible means to assess the defendant's comprehension of the Miranda rights.

## Questions Concerning the Interview

*Lying to the suspect about being taperecorded:*

Many state eavesdropping laws require only one-party consent. Under this circumstance, legally, the investigator may choose not to volunteer the fact that the interview or interrogation is being electronically recorded. There may be circumstances where the suspects asks whether or not the session is being electronically recorded and the investigator may decide to lie and deny that it is. A rational explanation for not being truthful to the suspect is a concern that informing him of the recording may inhibit the suspect's willingness to tell the truth. In addition, there may be a concern that the suspect will, "play up" to the camera.

*Interpreting the suspect's responses to behavior-provoking questions.*

The prosecution may be anxious for the jury to hear certain responses to behavior provoking questions asked during the interview because even common sense reveals that the answer suggests guilt. In doing so, however, the defense may then introduce other responses to behavior-provoking questions and ask the investigator to interpret those answers. Under this situation it is important for the witness to let the court know that the basis for forming an opinion is the preponderance of behavior occurring throughout the entire interview and that it may be very misleading to evaluate any particular behavior in isolation.

*Explaining the bait question:*

A bait question suggests the possible existence of evidence to entice the suspect to consider changing an earlier position, e.g., "Is there any reason why we would find your fingerprints inside that stolen car?" It is important that the investigator emphasize that this question is asked as a hypothetical one and the purpose for asking the bait question is to develop behavior symptoms of truth or deception and to assess the suspect's concern about the evidence existing. It is important that the court understand that 80% of deceptive suspects deny that the evidence will exist – it is the manner in which they offer this denial that is important to the investigator.

*Interpreting the suspect's nonverbal behavior:*

During almost any interview of a verified deceptive suspect, there will be portions where the suspect's nonverbal behavior appears truthful. The defense attorney may read a description of a truthful suspect's posture, hand movements and eye contact from our training manual and ask the witness if he agrees with that information. Once that foundation has been established, a portion of the defendant's interview may be played for the jury to view. Under this circumstance it is essential that the witness explain the importance of evaluating the preponderance of the suspect's behavior across the entire interview. It may also be that the portion of the interview selected involved investigative questions to which the suspect was telling the truth.

# Questions Concerning the Interrogation

*General concepts to keep in mind.*

During testimony the investigator should accurately use the terms interviewing and interrogation. Interrogation is not a dirty word and it is not illegal to interrogate criminal suspects. The investigator should not come across as apologetic when discussing interrogation. Whenever possible, the investigator should refer to eliciting the truth rather than eliciting a confession. For example, when describing why the interrogation was conducted in a particular manner it is preferable to refer to establishing an environment where the defendant was comfortable telling the truth as opposed to an environment in which the suspect would confess.

*Excessive length*

The defense attorney may attempt to greatly lengthen the actual time of an interrogation by including the duration of the interview as well as times involving no active persuasion (transportation to a particular facility, bathroom and lunch breaks, etc.). If the entire process is electronically recorded it should be possible to very accurately determine the time of the interrogation, e.g., Step One through Step Eight. On the other hand, if the investigator combines non-accusatory interviewing techniques with accusatory interrogation techniques, the defense calculation of the length of interrogation may be accurate.

*Explaining the Direct Positive Confrontation*

Most interrogations are conducted under a presumption that the suspect is guilty of the crime even though the investigator may not have any definite proof of that fact until after the suspect confesses. The investigator should openly acknowledge that at the outset of the interrogation he was not absolutely certain of the suspect's guilt. With respect to why the interrogation was conducted under a presumption of guilt, the witness may explain that experience has demonstrated that an investigator is much more likely to elicit the truth from a guilty suspect if the suspect believes that the investigator already knows the truth.

*Explaining Theme Development*

When the average attorney, judge or juror hears an interrogation theme they are taken aback. It does not conform to their expectation of what a police interrogation should be. The defense attorney may even suggest that the theme was an attempt to brainwash the suspect or plant seeds of guilt in his innocent client's mind. To respond effectively to these implications, it is essential that the investigator understand the psychology of theme development.

As part of the decision to commit a crime, the guilty suspect also justifies the crime. This justification may be in the form of projecting blame onto another person (the rape victim dressed provocatively, my friend talked me into stealing the car). The suspect may minimize the moral seriousness of the crime (at least there were no deaths in the arson fire), or rationalize the crime (the sexual contact with the child was done to show love and affection). These justifications already exist in the guilt suspect's mind and account for much of the documented differences between the innocent and guilty suspect's response to behavior-provoking questions during the interview. Consequently, the theme the investigator presents during the interrogation merely reinforces existing justifications. It is repeated and presented in a sympathetic manner in an effort to create an environment where the suspect feels comfortable telling the truth to the investigator. It is the goal of the interrogation to make it as psychologically easy as possible for the suspect to tell the truth.

*Explaining why the investigator dominates the conversation.*

The interrogation theme is presented in a monologue so as to discourage the suspect from offering denials. Each time the suspect denies involvement in the offense, it becomes more difficult psychologically for the suspect to tell the truth. In an effort to make it as psychologically easy as possible for the suspect to tell the truth, the investigator discourages the suspect's denials. If the suspect, in fact, is innocent of the crime, his denials will be vehement and persistent.

### *Explaining the investigator raising his voice*

An attempt will be made to argue that the investigator's increased volume (yelling) was designed to intimidate and frighten the suspect. The content of the statement, obviously will be important to consider. There are proper and improper reasons for an investigator to raise his voice. It is proper to speak loudly to a suspect in an effort to maintain the suspect's attention, e.g., "Mark! Listen to what I'm saying because this is important for you to know!" Similarly, it is generally an accepted interrogation tactic for the investigator to feign annoyance with the suspect. Under this circumstance the investigator may raise his voice and say, "Darn it Jim, you're not listening to a word I'm saying. I thought you cared about this thing but I guess I was wrong about you. You probably don't care about anything!" Following this feigned outburst, the investigator then apologizes for "losing his temper." In both of these situations, the investigator's raised voice is part of a purposeful and deliberate tactic. It is certainly not to the investigator's benefit to testify that he raised his voice as a result of uncontrollable anger toward the suspect. When the investigator testifies, in essence, that he was not in control of his emotions during the interrogation, the possibility of implied threats becomes more credible.

*Explaining false statements*

False statements run the continuum of insincere flattery such as, "You strike me as a basically honest person" to outright fabrications such as, "Jim, we found your fingerprints in her bedroom." An investigator should openly acknowledge making false statements to a suspect during an interrogation. Under most circumstances, courts permit an investigator to engage in trickery and deceit, provided that the statement does not shock the conscience of the court or community. (See Chapter 3 for legal guidelines affecting trickery and deceit.) When the investigator is asked why he lied to the suspect, the explanation must make sense to the court. Essentially, false statements are made in an effort to increase the probability that the suspect will tell the truth. Some false statements enhance the perception that the investigator understands and cares about the suspect; other false statements are designed to enhance the suspect's credibility.

*Allegations of a promise of leniency*

Especially with electronically recorded interrogations, a defense attorney may focus on a particular phrase and argue that it constituted a promise of leniency. Examples of these include, "The best thing you can do is to confess,"; "It would be far better for you if you confessed," or, "I want to be able to help you out on this thing but I can't help you unless you help me by telling me what happened." If the investigator happens to make a statement similar to these during an interrogation, hopefully it will be followed with a prophylactic statement such as, "Understand, that I am in no position to tell you what might happen to you if you tell me you did this." The defense attorney, of course, will not play that portion of the interrogation to the jury and the investigator's testimony must alert the court that a prophylactic statement was made.

In some interrogations there is no veiled promise of leniency mentioned at all, yet because of the investigator's sympathetic and understanding demeanor, the defense attorney may argue that his client came to believe that if he confessed he would be afforded leniency. Under this circumstance the investigator should essentially agree with the attorney's supposition by stating, "I am not surprised that the defendant felt that way. Because the defendant felt that his crime was somewhat justified, at least in his own mind, it would be natural for him to believe that he deserved some special consideration, including a reduced sentence."

*Moving closer to the suspect*

While procuring the suspect's attention in Step Five, it is recommended that the investigator gradually move his chair to a distance of approximately one foot directly in front of the suspect. The psychology of social spacing indicates that the zone of $1 - 1\frac{1}{2}$ feet is called the intimate zone and the only individuals comfortably allowed into that zone are highly trusted individuals such as family members or good friends. If a stranger enters a person's intimate zone, the immediate response is distrust and a feeling of being manipulated. The reason the investigator gradually attempts to move into the suspect's intimate zone is to enhance his credibility. In other words, if the suspect allows that close proxemics, the investigator will be afforded the same level of trust and sincerity the suspect would give a family member or friend.

*Explaining the alternative question*

A defense attorney may suggest that the investigator's use of an alternative question forced the defendant to confess because accepting either of the presented alternative choices represented an admission of guilt. The investigator should explain that the suspect had a third option, which is to reject both of the presented choices. Consider the alternative question, "Did you plan this out for months in advance or did it happen on the spur-of-the-moment?" Under this circumstance the suspect certainly has the choice to explain to the investigator that neither choice is correct because he did not commit the crime at all.

# Questions Concerning the Confession

*How do you know the confession is the truth?*

The best response to a question relating to the trustworthiness of a confession is to cite dependent and independent corroboration. In the absence of corroboration, the investigator may respond by saying, "I didn't do or say anything that would cause an innocent person to confess."

*Inaccurate information within the confession*

It is a rare occurrence for a guilty suspect to offer a confession that is 100% truthful and complete. The most common occurrence of this involves lies of omission. In other words, the investigator asks the suspect what he spent the stolen money on and the suspect states, "I can't remember. Just on stuff in general." In actuality, this suspect may have spent the money on drugs or gambling but he does not want to reveal that truth to the investigator so he lies by omission. The investigator should always accept the probability of lies of omission and never testify that the defendant's confession is totally accurate and complete. An effective statement to make in this regard is that the confession represents an accurate account of what the defendant was willing to reveal about his crime.

A more significant problem can arise when the defense attorney is able to demonstrate lies of commission within a confession. In an actual example of this, a juvenile suspect confessed to robbing a convenience store. When the investigator attempted to develop details of the confession, the suspect was reluctant to answer questions about how he left the scene. The investigator responded aggressively and continually demanded an answer to the question. The suspect finally stated that after the robbery he ran out of the store, down an alley and eventually went to his parent's home. These details were included in the written confession the suspect signed. During the suppression hearing the defense produced two eyewitnesses who testified that the young man who robbed the store left on a bicycle. Under this circumstance, the investigator does not have many options except to testify that despite erroneous details within the confession, he is still of the opinion that the defendant told the truth when he admitted committing the crime.

# Conclusion

Electronic recording of an interrogation and confession is a double edged sword. The same videotape that documents a suspect's Miranda waiver and refutes an allegation that physical force was used to obtain a confession, also reveals the various tactics and techniques the investigator used to persuade the suspect to tell the truth. Many of these procedures do not conform to an average juror's perception of what a police interrogation should be. This apparent discrepancy leaves the door wide open for a defense attorney to attack legitimate and legal interrogation procedures. Consequently, when testifying in a case where the interrogation and confession were electronically recorded the investigator must go beyond simply reporting the basic facts. Under this circumstance the investigator must also educate the court to explain why certain procedures were used and be prepared to explain why the procedures would not be apt to cause an innocent person to confess.

The effects of electronically recording interviews and interrogations are far reaching. They not only include establishing interview rooms to accommodate recording, understanding the legal requirements regulating electronic recording, maintaining the integrity of the recorded interview and interrogation as evidence but also developing an expertise in presenting the evidence in a court of law. In our experience with conducting training seminars we have encountered many successful interrogators who instinctively seem to know what to do and say to get suspects to confess. It is perhaps this type of "natural" interrogator who will experience the most difficulty testifying in a case where the interrogation and confession was electronically recorded. Conversely, an investigator who has received training in interviewing and interrogation techniques that not only covers how to conduct these procedures but also presents the underlying theories as to why these procedures are utilized, will be in an excellent position to educate the court during their testimony.

# Appendix A

## EMPIRICAL EXPERIENCES OF REQUIRED ELECTRONIC RECORDING OF INTERVIEWS AND INTERROGATIONS ON INVESTIGATORS' PRACTICES AND CASE OUTCOMES

*Brian C. Jayne*

## Abstract

The states of Alaska and Minnesota have required electronic recordings of custodial interviews and interrogations for more than a decade. The survey results of 112 investigators from those states indicate that a higher confession rate was obtained when suspects could not see the recording device during an interrogation. Furthermore, respondents believed that electronic recording generally decreases the length of a trial and that the practice does not benefit the defense. A significant endorsement of required electronic recording in custodial situations is that 85% of investigators either strongly favor the law or believe the law has not affected their ability to do their job.

## Introduction

In recent years defendants convicted of serious crimes have had their convictions overturned as a result of exculpatory evidence. A number of these individuals confessed following police interrogations, which has sparked controversy about interrogation practices. Some academicians have strongly advocated electronic recording of interviews and interrogations as a safeguard against false confessions.[70] There are also individuals who have expressed a belief that the interrogation techniques taught by John E. Reid and Associates are coercive and that the use of these techniques results in false confessions. Gudjonsson writes, "The experiments of Kassin and McNall are important because they show that the techniques advocated by Inbau and his colleagues are inherently coercive in that they communicate implicit threats and promises to suspects."[71] A vocal critic of the Reid Technique (Ofshe) goes so far as to allege that when using this technique, "Police routinely elicit false confessions."[72]

Almost across the board, federal agencies do not electronically record interviews or interrogations. Barring an all-encompassing U.S. Supreme Court decision, it would appear that the required recording of interviews and interrogations will be decided on a state-by-state basis. The first state to require electronic recording of interviews and interrogations was Alaska.[73] Nine years later Minnesota followed suit.[74] This year, at least two other states have introduced and/or passed similar legislation requiring electronic recording of all interrogations.

---

[70] Gudjonsson, G.(2003) The Psychology of Interrogations and Confessions Wiley & Sons, West Sussex, 21-24.

[71] Kassin McNall, (1991) "Police Interrogations and Confessions: Communicating Promises and Threats by Pragmatic Implication," *Law and Human Behavior* 15, 3, 233-25.

[72] *Supra* note 1, p. 21

[73] Stephan v. State, 711 P.2d1156, 1158 Alaska, 1985.

[74] State v. Scales, 518 N.W. 2d 587 Minnesota, 1994. In a recent case (State v. Conger, Minnesota, 2002) the Supreme Court refused to expand required electronic recording to non-custodial interviews and interrogations.

There has been scant research in the area of electronic recordings of interviews, interrogations or confessions. The most detailed attempt at this effort was a 1992 National Institute of Justice (NIJ) study that surveyed about 2,400 law enforcement agencies across the United States.[7] This report indicated that only 16 percent of the agencies surveyed videotaped interviews, interrogations or confessions. The reported benefits of videotaping confessions were 1) to minimize doubts as to the trustworthiness or voluntariness of a confession, 2) to help an investigator prepare for testimony and, 3) to defend against allegations of improper interrogation tactics. The majority of agencies surveyed did not videotape interviews, interrogations or confessions. There were two primary reasons cited for this. One was a concern that the recording would increase defense claims of improper interrogation tactics and a second was a belief that videotaping the interrogation would inhibit a suspect's willingness to tell the truth.

While the NIJ report provides a baseline of law enforcement recording practices, the methodology omitted some significant variables relative to electronic recording. First, the study focused only on videotaped recordings. Second, there was a failure to identify whether or not agencies recorded the entire interview and interrogation of a suspect or just the suspect's confession. Finally, most agencies surveyed indicated that they selectively videotaped only certain cases. Despite these shortcomings, the NIJ report is significant in that it serves as a barometer of the attitudes and concerns toward electronic recording by law enforcement agencies that existed in 1992.

To fully understand the implication of electronic recordings of police interactions with subjects, a distinction must be made between an interview, an interrogation and a confession. An interview is a non-accusatory question-and-answer session with a person who may have useful information about a crime under investigation. This person may be a witness, an informant, an individual with helpful knowledge or a suspect. Some interviews result in confessions or incriminating statements. In other situations, the person may be cleared of any wrongdoing. If the person being interviewed is a suspect he may or may not be placed in custody.

An *interrogation* describes an accusatory interaction with a suspect believed to be involved in a crime. Through active persuasive, the investigator attempts to convince the suspect to tell the truth using arguments that are based on factual or emotional elements of the crime. An interrogation may result in a confession, a partial admission or, when the suspect does not make any incriminating statements, an increased belief of his probable involvement in the crime. Some interrogations may produce the opposite result, where the investigator accepts the suspect's denials as truthful statements. A suspect may or may not be taken into custody prior to an interrogation.

A *confession* is a statement acknowledging commission of a crime coupled with information about the crime that would only be known by the guilty person and/or that can be independently verified following the confession. An unsupported statement such as, "I didn't intend on killing him," "I'm sorry I did this," or "I lied about my alibi" is not a confession. A confession may be offered by a suspect who is either in custody or not in custody.

Because of the potential impact electronic recording of interviews or interrogations may have on an investigator's ability to perform his duties and on the criminal justice system itself, there is much controversy surrounding the practice. A unique opportunity, however, exists which may provide meaningful data and insight on this important issue. Investigators working in Alaska and Minnesota have had many years of experience working within the constraints of these laws. Consequently, it was believed that these investigators would be in the best position to offer real-life experiences with electronic recording of interviews and interrogations.

# Methodology / Sample

### Data Sheet

Eight hundred questionnaires were mailed to police investigators in the states of Alaska and Minnesota who had received training in The Reid Technique of Interviewing and Interrogation within the last two years. The questionnaire requested no personal information and was, therefore, anonymous. Respondents mailed the questionnaires to the author who entered their answers into a database file for analysis.

One of the reasons this sample included only investigators who received training in the Reid Technique is that the training emphasizes the distinctions between interviewing and interrogation and also clearly defines terms such as "admission" and "confession." By selecting a sample of investigators who all shared the same training in interviewing and interrogation it was believed that the data would most accurately reflect the questions asked on the survey.

<u>Sample</u>

Out of the 800 surveys, 112 investigators responded, representing a 14% return. Thirty-four of these were from Alaska and 78 from Minnesota. The sample included responses from 21 different agencies in Alaska and 53 agencies from Minnesota. The average number of years employed in law enforcement for the sample was 8.9 years, with a range from one to 24 years. Over the last two years these investigators conducted an estimated total of 9,375 interviews and 5,651 interrogations.

# Results

<u>Recording Practices</u>

The laws regulating electronic recording of interviews and interrogations in Alaska and Minnesota do not specify the type of recording to be made. Therefore, it was of interest to determine if there was a preference for either audio or audiovisual recordings. Table 1 lists these preferences.

Table 1

Type of Electronic Recording Generally Made

| Type of Recording | N | (%) |
|---|---|---|
| Audio | 83 | (74%) |
| Audiovisual | 18 | (16%) |
| Half Audio, Half Audiovisual | 11 | (10%) |

In Alaska and Minnesota only custodial interviews or interrogations are required to be recorded. An investigator often has a choice as to whether to conduct a voluntary, non-custodial interview or, conversely, to take a suspect into custody before conducting the interview and interrogation. It was speculated that investigators may try to minimize the impact of the law by increasing the number of suspects who are interviewed or interrogated in a non-custodial environment. A specific question was asked in this survey to identify whether or not investigators bypassed the electronic recording requirement by more frequently conducting non-custodial interviews/interrogations. Those results are listed in Table 2. Respondents were also asked to estimate the frequency in which they record interviews and interrogations. Table 3 lists those findings.

## Table 2

### Effect Required Recording Has on Increasing Non-Custodial Interviews/Interrogations

| How much have you increased the number of non-custodial interviews/interrogations? | N | (%) |
|---|---|---|
| Significantly | 83 | (74%) |
| Somewhat | 18 | (16%) |
| Not at all | 11 | (10%) |

## Table 3

### Frequencies of Recording Interviews and Interrogations

| % Frequency of Recording | During an Interview | During an Interrogation |
|---|---|---|
| 0 - 20% | 3  (  2%) | 0  (  0%) |
| 20 - 40% | 4  (  4%) | 2  (  2%) |
| 40 - 60% | 5  (  5%) | 3  (  3%) |
| 60 - 80% | 10  (  9%) | 5  (  4%) |
| 80 -100% | 90  (80%) | 102  (91%) |

As these results indicate, investigators in Alaska and Minnesota electronically record the majority of their interviews and almost all of their interrogations, even though this is required only when a suspect is in custody.[8]  Furthermore, the majority of investigators did not make a significant effort to avoid electronic recording by increasing the number of non-custodial interviews or interrogations conducted.

Effect on Confessions

One of the primary concerns expressed by law enforcement relating to electronic recording of interviews or interrogations is that the suspect's knowledge that his statements are being recorded would inhibit the truth-seeking process.  In the NIJ report 30% of agencies who chose not to videotape interviews or interrogations cited this as a primary concern. From a psychological perspective it must be appreciated that it is not the electronic recording of interviews or interrogations that potentially inhibits truthfulness; it is the suspect's knowledge and awareness of being electronically recorded.  An obvious solution to this dilemma is surreptitious recording without the suspect's knowledge.

In Alaska and Minnesota, an investigator is not required to advise a suspect that his statements are being electronically recorded and also has the option to hide the recording device during an interview or interrogation. To determine the extent to which investigators took advantage of their ability to surreptitiously record interviews and interrogations one survey question addressed the frequency in which subjects were told that their conversation was being recorded. A second question asked about the frequency in which the recording device was visible to the subject. In this sample relatively few investigators attempted to surreptitiously record interviews or interrogations. These findings are listed in Table 4.

Table 4

How Often Subjects are Advised They are Being Recorded
And Can See the Recording Device

| Frequency | Advised they are recorded | Can see recording device |
|-----------|---------------------------|--------------------------|
| Never     | 26   (23%)                | 10    ( 9%)              |
| Sometimes | 35   (31%)                | 48    (43%)              |
| Usually   | 25   (23%)                | 30    (27%)              |
| Always    | 26   (23%)                | 24    (21%)              |

To investigate the effect electronic recordings have on the frequency in which investigators obtained confessions, both empirical and objective data was generated. Respondents were asked how they believed electronic recording affected their rate of eliciting confessions both during an interview and interrogation. These results are listed in Table 5.

## Table 5

### Experience of Electronic Recording on Confessions
### During Interviews and Interrogations

| Observation | Interview | Interrogation |
|---|---|---|
| Not affected number of confessions | 85  (76%) | 82  (74%) |
| Decreased number of confessions | 20  (18%) | 25  (22%) |
| Increased number of confessions | 7  ( 6%) | 4  ( 4%) |

An important variable to consider with respect to electronic recordings and confession rates is the suspect's knowledge of being electronically recorded. Clearly, the greatest reminder of this is having the recording device visible. Table 6 reflects the reported confessions rates during an interrogation ranging from never having the recording device visible to always having the recording device visible.

## Table 6

### Effect of Visibility of Recording Device on Confession Rates

| Condition | Confession Rate |
|---|---|
| Never Visible | 82% |
| Sometimes Visible | 52% |
| Usually Visible | 50% |
| Always Visible | 43% |

While the majority of investigators (74%) reported that they believed electronic recording did not affect their ability to elicit the truth during an interrogation, Table 6 indicates that when a subject is not able to see the recording device, confession rates are much higher than when the recording device is always visible. While correlation coefficients were not calculated because of the of nature of data collected, the gradual decrease of confession rates illustrated in Table 6 suggests a significant relationship between the number of suspects who confess and the lack of visibility of a recording devise.

Effects on Trial

A concern some agencies have with electronically recording interviews and interrogations is that the practice provides the defense with unnecessarily detailed material which could be used to suppress an otherwise legally admissible confession or to bog down the court system with a prolonged suppression hearing. The NIJ report indicated an 18% increase in defense claims of improper interrogation techniques when the interrogation was videotaped. The remaining 82% of agencies reported that defense claims stayed the same or decreased. In this study investigators were asked whether electronic recording of interviews and interrogations most favored the prosecution or defense. Table 7 indicates the results of the respondents' experience.

## Table 7

Effects of Electronic Recording on the Adversarial System

| Observation | N | ( %) |
|---|---|---|
| Most benefits the prosecution | 54 | (48%) |
| Most benefits the defense | 8 | ( 7%) |
| Benefits the prosecution and defense equally | 50 | (45%) |

Respondents were also asked to assess the effect electronic recording of interviews and interrogations has had on the length of a trial. The survey option indicating a decrease in trial length suggested such reasons as more plea bargains and shorter suppression hearings. The option indicating an increase in trial length suggested defense expert testimony and the time for the court to review the electronic recording. The results are listed in Table 8.

## Table 8

The Effects of Electronic Recording on the Length of Trial

| Observation | N | ( %) |
|---|---|---|
| Not affected the length of trial | 28 | (25%) |
| Decreased the length of trial | 76 | (68%) |
| Increased the length of trial | 8 | ( 7%) |

Tables 7 and 8 both reflect positive findings about electronic recording from a prosecution perspective. That is, electronic recording generally does not benefit the defense and also decreases the length of a trial. A number of the respondents wrote on their surveys that electronic recording of confessions significantly increased the number of plea bargains.

The survey specifically inquired about the number of confessions that were suppressed at trial. Of the 3,938 confessions obtained during an interview, 33 (.83%) were suppressed at trial. Twelve of these suppressed confessions were electronically recorded and 21 were not. The survey did not pursue the grounds for suppression. However, considering that two-thirds of these confessions were not electronically recorded suggests that the investigator believed that the suspect was not in custody at the time of questioning. It is, therefore, probable that many of these suppressed confessions involved either Miranda issues or state-imposed regulations, e.g., was the suspect in custody at the time of the questioning and, was therefore, electronic recording required?

Out of the reported 3,162 confessions obtained following an interrogation, 18 were suppressed at trial (.56%). Fourteen of these were electronically recorded and four were not.[9] Because the survey did not pursue grounds for suppression it is not known to what extent, if any, electronic recording contributed to the suppression of these confessions. It is important to remember that the vast majority of the 3,144 confessions that were not suppressed as evidence were electronically recorded (see Table 3).

An impressive statistic that can be drawn from this finding is that 99.44% of confessions obtained during an interrogation were not suppressed even though the vast majority of them were electronically recorded and, in those cases, the defense was able to scrutinize every word of the interrogation. Considering that all of these investigators received training in the Reid Technique and presumably used that technique, at least in part, to obtain these confessions offers a strong challenge to opponents' claims that the Reid Technique is inherently coercive and results in false confessions.

## Discussion

Investigators who responded to this survey offered real-life experiences of mandated recording of custodial interviews and interrogations which should serve as a valuable source of information to states considering similar legislation. The clear preference for electronic recording is audiotaping versus audiovisual recording. This may be due to cost or convenience factors. While some opponents of police interrogation advocate audiovisual recordings, this medium may involve perceptual problems that potentially could result in longer and more confusing trials.10 Overall, investigators in Alaska and Minnesota have adapted their interviewing and interrogation practices to accommodate the recording laws, as 80% indicated that they electronically record 80-100% of their interviews and 91% indicated recording 80-100% of interrogations. Only 8% of investigators reported legally evading the law by increasing the number of non-custodial interviews or interrogations they conduct.

A significant part of an investigator's job involves gathering information and evidence through interviews and interrogations. While 74% of investigators in this study did not believe that electronic recording affected their ability to elicit confessions, objective findings challenge this perception. Investigators who never allowed subjects to see the recording device during an interrogation achieved a 39% higher confession rate than investigators who always had the recording device visible. This finding suggests that a suspect who is aware that a conversation is being recorded may be less likely to be forthright. Another possibility is that more skilled interrogators have learned not to make the recording device visible to suspects. Because of the general nature of data collected, this must be considered a preliminary finding and deserves further research. In the meantime, it may be prudent for investigators to make an attempt to surreptitiously record interviews and interrogations.

Another significant issue relating to altering police procedures is the effect those changes have on the court system. Investigators in this sample did not believe that electronic recording provided an unfair advantage to the defense. In fact, 48% believed that it favored the prosecution. A coinciding finding is that 68% of investigators believed that electronic recording decreased the length of a trial. At first blush this may appear to be a very positive finding. However, this is only true if electronically recorded interrogations and confessions serve to efficiently resolve common suppression hearing disputes, such as whether or not the suspect was given his Miranda warnings or to refute claims of alleged threats or promises. The other possibility is that an electronically recorded interrogation and confession is considered so damaging that an average defendant feels powerless to refute it and pleads guilty. Further research in this area is certainly warranted.

The total number of reported confessions that were suppressed was so small that no meaningful statistical analysis can be made. Combining confessions from interviews and interrogations, a total of 51 (.71%)

confessions were suppressed. Of these, 26 were electronically recorded and 25 were not. It would be interesting to pursue this statistic further. For example, do states that require electronic recording have a greater or lesser rate of suppressed confessions than states that do not? Are the grounds for suppressing confessions in states that require electronic recording different from states that do not? Because of the specific standard of requiring electronic recordings in only custodial situations, common sense indicates that defense attorneys may focus on the suspect's state of mind at the time a confession was given, e.g., did the defendant believe he was in custody and, therefore, the session would be electronically recorded? In this regard, it would be to the investigator's advantage to clearly advise a non-custodial suspect that he is not under arrest and is free to leave at any time.

The final consideration when enacting legislation that alters existing procedures is how the people affected will respond to the change. To address this, a question was asked on the survey as to the impact required recording has had on the investigator's job. The results are listed in Table 9. As can be seen, the vast majority of investigators in this study either strongly support electronic recording or believe that it has not affected their ability to do their job.

## Table 9

### Investigator's Opinion of Requiring Electronic Recording of Interviews and Interrogations

| Opinion | N ( %) |
|---|---|
| Support the law and believe it should be passed in other states | 53 (47%) |
| Not affected by the law one way or another | 42 (38%) |
| The law has decreased the investigator's ability to perform duties | 12 (11%) |
| The law is wrong and should be repealed | 5 ( 4%) |

In conclusion, much of the law enforcement concern surrounding electronic recording of interviews, interrogations and confessions described in the 1992 NIJ study appears to be unwarranted. In actual practice, a preponderance of investigators report no overwhelming negative effects associated with required electronic recording and generally express positive experiences. This reform in interviewing and interrogation practices suggests that the requirement of electronic recording in custodial cases is not only feasible, but may have an overall benefit to the criminal justice system. In an era where academicians generalize from laboratory studies and use anecdotal accounts to support claims that police routinely elicit false confessions, electronic recordings may be the most effective means to dispel these unsupported notions.

# Appendix B

## DEPARTMENTS THAT CURRENTLY RECORD CUSTODIAL INTERROGATIONS[75]

| LAW ENFORCEMENT AGENCY | POPULATION (2000 CENSUS) | SWORN OFFICERS | AUDIO/ VIDEO | YEARS RECORDING |
|---|---|---|---|---|
| **Alaska** | | | | |
| All agencies | 626,932 | | A/V | 19 |
| **Arizona** | | | | |
| Casa Grande PD | 25,224 | 60 | A/V | 10+ |
| Chandler PD | 176,581 | 304 | A/V | 20+ |
| Coconino County SO | 116,320 | 64 | A/V | 15+ |
| El Mirage PD | 7,609 | 47 | A/V | 1+ |
| Flagstaff PD | 52,894 | 95 | A/V | 6 |
| Gila County SO | 51,335 | 52 | A/V | 5 |
| Gilbert PD | 109,697 | 151 | A/V | 8 |
| Glendale PD | 218,812 | 300 | A/V | 10 |
| Marana PD | 13,556 | 65 | A | 9+ |
| Maricopa County SO | 3,072,149 | 675 | A/V | 10+ |
| Mesa PD | 396,375 | 820 | A/V | 12+ |
| Oro Valley PD | 29,700 | 75 | A/V | 10+ |
| Payson PD | 13,620 | 28 | A/V | 11+ |
| Peoria PD | 108,364 | 155 | A/V | 5 |
| Phoenix PD | 1,321,045 | 2,400 | A/V | 2+ |
| Pima County SO | 843,746 | 450 | A/V | 12 |
| Pinal County SO | 179,727 | 150 | A/V | |
| Prescott PD | 33,938 | 63 | A/V | 12 |
| Scottsdale PD | 202,705 | 300 | A/V | 10 |
| Somerton PD | 7,266 | 16 | A/V | 8 |
| South Tucson PD | 5,490 | 27 | A | 10 |

---

[75] This table was reprinted from the Sullivan Report on Police Experiences with Recording Custodial Interrogations, Northwestern University No. 1 2004.
The complete report and its appendices are posted on the Internet at:
http://www.law.northwestern.edu/wrongfulconvictions/Causes/Custodial Interrogations.htm

| LAW ENFORCEMENT AGENCY | POPULATION (2000 CENSUS) | SWORN OFFICERS | AUDIO/ VIDEO | YEARS RECORDING |
|---|---|---|---|---|
| Somerton PD | 7,266 | 16 | A/V | 8 |
| South Tucson PD | 5,490 | 27 | A | 10 |
| Surprise PD | 30,848 | 85 | A/V | 20+ |
| Tempe PD | 158,625 | 380 | A/V | 5 |
| Tucson PD | 486,699 | 943 | A/V | 30+ |
| Yavapai County SO | 167,517 | 123 | A/V | 10+ |
| Yuma County SO | 160,026 | 80 | A | 5 |
| Yuma PD | 77,515 | 144 | A/V | 4 |
| **Arkansas** | | | | |
| 14th Judicial District Drug Task Force | | 4 | A/V | 10+ |
| Fayetteville PD | 58,047 | 140 | A/V | 5 |
| State Police | 2,673,400 | 490 | A | |
| Van Buren PD | 18,986 | 46 | A/V | 8+ |
| **California** | | | | |
| Alameda County SO | 1,443,741 | 1,000 | A/V | 10+ |
| Auburn PD | 12,462 | 25 | A/V | 15 |
| Butte County SO | 203,171 | 110 | A/V | 15 |
| Carlsbad PD | 78,247 | 107 | A/V | 20 |
| Contra Costa County SO | 948,816 | 850 | A/V | 10 |
| El Cajon PD | 94,869 | 155 | A | 25 |
| El Dorado County SO | 156,299 | 160 | A/V | 10 |
| Escondido PD | 133,559 | 168 | A/V | 20+ |
| Folsom PD | 51,884 | 73 | A/V | 10 |
| Grass Valley PD | 10,922 | 29 | A/V | 5 |
| Hayward PD | 140,030 | 225 | A/V | 14 |
| La Mesa PD | 54,749 | 66 | A/V | 9+ |
| Livermore PD | 73,345 | 97 | A/V | 20 |
| Los Angeles PD | 3,694,820 | 7,000 | A | 23 |

| LAW ENFORCEMENT AGENCY | POPULATION (2000 CENSUS) | SWORN OFFICERS | AUDIO/ VIDEO | YEARS RECORDING |
|---|---|---|---|---|
| Oceanside PD | 161,029 | 200 | A/V | 15 |
| Orange County SO | 2,846,289 | 1,600 | A/V | 15+ |
| Placer County SO | 248,399 | 250 | A/V | 10 |
| Rocklin PD | 36,330 | 45 | A/V | 12+ |
| Roseville PD | 79,921 | 110 | A/V | 10+ |
| Sacramento County SO | 1,223,499 | 1,700 | A/V | 25 |
| Sacramento PD | 407,018 | 675 | A/V | 22+ |
| San Bernardino SO | 1,709,434 | 1,550 | A/V | 25 |
| San Diego PD | 1,223,400 | 2,100 | A/V | 15+ |
| San Francisco PD | 776,733 | 2,500 | A/V | |
| San Joaquin County SO | 563,598 | 250 | A/V | 20+ |
| San Jose PD | 894,943 | 1,400 | A/V | 25+ |
| San Leandro PD | 79,452 | 94 | A/V | 15 |
| San Luis PD | 44,174 | 32 | A | 8 |
| Santa Clara County SO | 1,682,585 | 635 | A/V | |
| Santa Clara PD | 102,361 | 140 | A/V | 20+ |
| Santa Cruz PD | 54,593 | 95 | A/V | 4+ |
| Stockton PD | 243,771 | 372 | A/V | 8+ |
| Union City PD | 66,869 | 72 | A/V | 16 |
| Ventura County SO | 753,197 | 850 | A/V | 30 |
| West Sacramento PD | 31,615 | 62 | A/V | 5 |
| Woodland PD | 49,151 | 600 | A/V | 5 |
| Yolo County SO | 168,660 | 100 | A/V | 15 |
| **Colorado** | | | | |
| Arvada PD | 102,153 | 140 | A/V | 17 |
| Aurora PD | 276,283 | 570 | A/V | 8+ |
| Boulder PD | 94,673 | 163 | A/V | 10 |
| Brighton PD | 20,905 | 53 | A/V | 2 |
| Broomfield PD | 38,272 | 130 | A/V | 9 |
| Colorado Springs PD | 360,890 | 686 | A/V | 7+ |

| LAW ENFORCEMENT AGENCY | POPULATION (2000 CENSUS) | SWORN OFFICERS | AUDIO/ VIDEO | YEARS RECORDING |
|---|---|---|---|---|
| Commerce City PD | 20,991 | 75 | A/V | 15 |
| Denver PD | 554,636 | 1,300 | A/V | 22 |
| El Paso County SO | 516,929 | 386 | A/V | 17 |
| Ft. Collins PD | 118,652 | 156 | A/V | 20 |
| Lakewood PD | 144,126 | 270 | A/V | 10 |
| Larimer County SO | 251,494 | 237 | A/V | 25+ |
| Loveland PD | 50,608 | 79 | A/V | 9+ |
| Sterling PD | 11,360 | 22 | A | 5+ |
| Thornton PD | 82,384 | 147 | A/V | 8 |
| **Connecticut** | | | | |
| Bloomfield PD | 19,587 | 52 | A/V | 2 |
| Cheshire PD | 28,543 | 48 | A/V | 20 |
| **District of Columbia** | | | | |
| Metropolitan PD | 572,059 | 3,700 | A/V | 1 |
| **Florida** | | | | |
| Broward County SO | 1,623,018 | 2,000 | A/V | 1 |
| Collier County SO | 251,377 | 800 | A/V | 6 |
| Coral Springs PD | 117,549 | 200 | A/V | 7 |
| Daytona Beach PD | 64,112 | 245 | A/V | 25 |
| Ft. Lauderdale PD | 152,397 | 500 | A/V | 1 |
| Hallandale Beach PD | 34,282 | 95 | A/V | 6 months |
| Hialeah PD | 226,419 | 300 | A | 20+ |
| Hollywood PD | 139,357 | 340 | A/V | 1 |
| Kissimmee PD | 47,814 | 140 | A/V | 8+ |
| Manatee County SO | 264,002 | 650 | A/V | 20 |
| Miami PD | 362,470 | 1,100 | A/V | 1+ |
| Mount Dora PD | 9,418 | 36 | A/V | 18 |
| Orange County SO | 896,344 | 1,500 | A/V | 22 |
| Osceola County SO | 172,493 | 400 | A/V | 15 |
| Palatka PD | 10,033 | 35 | A/V | 6+ |
| Pembroke Pines PD | 137,427 | 225 | A/V | 2+ |

| LAW ENFORCEMENT AGENCY | POPULATION (2000 CENSUS) | SWORN OFFICERS | AUDIO/ VIDEO | YEARS RECORDING |
|---|---|---|---|---|
| Pinellas County SO | 921,482 | 900 | A/V | 20 |
| Port Orange PD | 45,823 | 82 | A/V | 20 |
| St. Petersburg PD | 248,232 | 539 | A/V | 5+ |
| **Georgia** | | | | |
| Atlanta PD | 416,474 | 1,500 | A/V | |
| Cobb County PD | 607,751 | 558 | A/V | 20+ |
| DeKalb County PD | 665,865 | 1,000 | A/V | 2 |
| Fulton County PD | 816,006 | 350 | A/V | 8+ |
| Gwinnett County PD | 588,448 | 515 | A/V | 15 |
| Macon PD | 97,255 | 305 | A/V | 15+ |
| Savannah-Chatham PD | 232,048 | 600 | A/V | 10 |
| **Hawaii** | | | | |
| Honolulu PD | 371,657 | 1,200 | A | 18+ |
| **Idaho** | | | | |
| Coeur d'Alene PD | 34,514 | 63 | A/V | 16+ |
| Dep't. of Fish & Games | 1,341,131 | 100 | A | 10+ |
| Jerome PD | 7,780 | 20 | A/V | 6 |
| Nampa PD | 51,867 | 95 | A/V | 4+ |
| **Illinois**[1] | | | | |
| DuPage County SO | 904,161 | 439 | A/V | 4 |
| East St. Louis PD | 31,542 | 65 | A/V | |
| Kankakee County SO | 103,833 | 63 | A/V | 10 |
| Kankakee PD | 27,491 | 71 | A/V | 10 |
| Naperville PD | 128,358 | 182 | A/V | 8 |
| O'Fallon PD | 21,910 | 43 | A/V | 1 |
| **Indiana** | | | | |
| Auburn PD | 12,074 | 22 | A/V | 7 |
| Carmel PD | 37,733 | 90 | A/V | 15+ |

| LAW ENFORCEMENT AGENCY | POPULATION (2000 CENSUS) | SWORN OFFICERS | AUDIO/ VIDEO | YEARS RECORDING |
|---|---|---|---|---|
| Cicero PD | 4,303 | 7 | A/V | 3 |
| Elkhart PD | 51,874 | 118 | A/V | 15 |
| Fishers PD | 37,835 | 69 | A/V | 8 |
| Ft. Wayne PD | 205,727 | 400 | A/V | 20+ |
| Greensburg PD | 10,260 | 18 | A/V | 20 |
| Hamilton County SO | 182,740 | 60 | A/V | 12+ |
| Hancock County SO | 55,391 | 40 | A/V | 7 |
| Johnson County SO | 115,209 | 60 | A/V | 4 |
| Noblesville PD | 28,590 | 67 | A/V | 5 |
| Sheridan PD | 2,520 | 5 | A/V | 16 |
| Steuben County SO | 33,214 | 21 | A/V | 5 |
| Westfield PD | 9,293 | 30 | A/V | 10+ |
| **Iowa** | | | | |
| Sioux City PD | 85,013 | 127 | A/V | 15 |
| **Kansas** | | | | |
| Sedgwick County SO | 452,869 | 172 | A/V | 20+ |
| Wichita PD | 344,284 | 650 | A/V | 5 |
| **Kentucky** | | | | |
| Elizabethtown PD | 22,542 | 42 | A/V | 5+ |
| Hardin County SO | 94,174 | 20 | A/V | 2 |
| Oldham County SO | 46,178 | 30 | A/V | 4 |
| **Louisiana** | | | | |
| Lafayette City PD | 110,257 | 240 | A/V | 15 |
| Lake Charles PD | 71,757 | 175 | A/V | 10 |
| Plaquemines Parish SO | 26,757 | 216 | A | 19 |
| St. Tammany Parish SO | 191,268 | 600 | A/V | 7+ |
| **Maine** | | | | |
| Lewiston PD | 35,690 | 80 | A/V | 15 |
| Portland PD | 64,249 | 160 | A/V | 2 |
| State Police | 1,274,923 | 320 | A/V | 15 |
| **Maryland** | | | | |

| LAW ENFORCEMENT AGENCY | POPULATION (2000 CENSUS) | SWORN OFFICERS | AUDIO/ VIDEO | YEARS RECORDING |
|---|---|---|---|---|
| Harford County SO | 218,590 | 685 | A/V | 15 |
| Prince George's County PD | 801,515 | 1,420 | A/V | 2 |
| **Massachusetts** | | | | |
| Yarmouth PD | 24,807 | 52 | A/V | 2+ |
| **Michigan** | | | | |
| Kentwood PD | 45,255 | 72 | A/V | 10 |
| Ludington PD | 8,357 | 14 | A/V | 3 |
| Waterford PD | 73,150 | 90 | A/V | 5+ |
| **Minnesota** | | | | |
| All agencies | 4,919,479 | | A/V | 10 |
| **Mississippi** | | | | |
| Biloxi PD | 50,644 | 145 | A/V | 25 |
| Cleveland | 13,841 | 40 | A | 20 |
| Gulfport PD | 71,127 | 200 | A/V | 15 |
| Harrison County SO | 189,601 | 250 | A/V | 5 |
| Jackson County SO | 131,420 | 150 | A/V | 19 |
| **Missouri** | | | | |
| St. Louis County Major Case Squad | 1,016,315 | | A/V | |
| St. Louis County PD | 1,016,315 | 730 | A/V | |
| **Montana** | | | | |
| Billings PD | 89,847 | 128 | A/V | 20 |
| Bozeman PD | 27,509 | 42 | A | 18 |
| Butte/Silverbow LED | 34,606 | 40 | A/V | 10+ |
| Cascade County SO | 80,357 | 40 | A/V | 10+ |
| Flathead County SO | 74,471 | 45 | A/V | 10+ |
| Gallatin County SO | 67,831 | 40 | A | 10+ |
| Great Falls PD | 56,690 | 80 | A/V | 8 |
| Helena PD | 25,780 | 49 | A/V | 10 |

| LAW ENFORCEMENT AGENCY | POPULATION (2000 CENSUS) | SWORN OFFICERS | AUDIO/ VIDEO | YEARS RECORDING |
|---|---|---|---|---|
| Kalispell PD | 14,223 | 45 | A/V | 10+ |
| Lewis & Clark County SO | 55,716 | 40 | A/V | 15 |
| Missoula PD | 57,053 | 89 | A/V | 3 |
| Missoula County SO | 95,802 | 58 | A/V | 14 |
| **Nebraska** | | | | |
| Douglas County SO | 463,585 | 120 | A/V | 20 |
| Lancaster County SO | 250,291 | 73 | A/V | 3 |
| Lincoln PD | 225,581 | 315 | A/V | 28 |
| Madison County SO | 35,226 | 23 | A/V | 2 |
| Norfolk PD | 23,816 | 43 | A/V | 6 |
| North Platte PD | 23,878 | 42 | A/V | 1 |
| Omaha PD | 390,007 | 750 | A/V | 8+ |
| O'Neill PD | 3,733 | 7 | A/V | 12 |
| Sarpy County SO | 122,595 | 123 | A/V | 20 |
| State Patrol | 1,711,263 | 509 | A/V | 10 |
| **Nevada** | | | | |
| Boulder City PD | 14,966 | 28 | A/V | 4 |
| Carlin PD | 2,161 | 6 | A/V | 10+ |
| Dep't. Public Safety | 1,998,257 | 49 | A | 16 |
| Douglas County SO | 41,259 | 97 | A/V | 12 |
| Elko County SO | 45,291 | 75 | A/V | 12 |
| Elko PD | 16,708 | 35 | A/V | 12 |
| Henderson PD | 175,381 | 280 | A/V | 10 |
| Lander County SO | 5,794 | 23 | A/V | 3 |
| Las Vegas Metro PD | 488,111 | 1,988 | A/V | 26 |
| North Las Vegas PD | 115,488 | 215 | A/V | 7+ |
| Reno PD | 180,480 | 300 | A/V | 25 |
| Sparks PD | 66,346 | 102 | A/V | 15+ |
| Washoe County SO | 339,486 | 400 | A/V | 20 |
| Wells PD | 1,346 | 52 | A/V | 8 |

| LAW ENFORCEMENT AGENCY | POPULATION (2000 CENSUS) | SWORN OFFICERS | AUDIO/ VIDEO | YEARS RECORDING |
|---|---|---|---|---|
| Yerington PD | 2,883 | 7 | A/V | 30 |
| **New Mexico** | | | | |
| Carlsbad PD | 25,625 | 50 | A | 5+ |
| Doña Ana County SO | 174,682 | 150 | A | 18 |
| Hobbs PD | 28,657 | 81 | A/V | 4 |
| Las Cruces PD | 74,267 | 150 | A/V | 18 |
| Santa Fe PD | 62,203 | 143 | A/V | 6 |
| **New York** | | | | |
| Broome County SO | 200,536 | 52 | A/V | 2+ |
| **Ohio** | | | | |
| Akron PD | 217,074 | 480 | A | 15 |
| Garfield Heights PD | 30,734 | 61 | A/V | 2 |
| Millersburg PD | 3,326 | 9 | A/V | 11 |
| Wapakoneta PD | 9,474 | 14 | A/V | 2 |
| Westlake PD | 31,719 | 40 | A/V | 10 |
| **Oklahoma** | | | | |
| Moore PD | 41,138 | 62 | A/V | 20 |
| Norman PD | 95,694 | 130 | A/V | 10 |
| Oklahoma County SO | 660,448 | 350 | A/V | 1 |
| Tecumseh PD | 6,098 | 10 | A/V | 5 |
| **Oregon** | | | | |
| Clackamas County SO | 338,391 | 300 | A | 5+ |
| Eugene PD | 137,893 | 175 | A/V | 26 |
| Medford PD | 63,154 | 97 | A/V | 16 |
| Portland PD | 529,121 | 1,048 | A/V | 15+ |
| Springfield Office, State Police | | 25 | A/V | |
| Warrenton PD | 4,096 | 8 | A/V | 6 months |
| Yamhill County SO | 84,992 | 40 | A/V | 6 |
| **South Dakota** | | | | |

| LAW ENFORCEMENT AGENCY | POPULATION (2000 CENSUS) | SWORN OFFICERS | AUDIO/ VIDEO | YEARS RECORDING |
|---|---|---|---|---|
| Aberdeen PD | 24,658 | 40 | A/V | 3+ |
| Brown County SO | 35,460 | 14 | A/V | 20 |
| **Tennessee** | | | | |
| Blount County SO | 105,823 | 300 | A/V | 20 |
| Chattanooga PD | 155,554 | 480 | A | 2 |
| Loudon County SO | 4,476 | 35 | A | 2 |
| **Texas** | | | | |
| Austin PD | 656,562 | 1,431 | A/V | 5+ |
| Cleburne PD | 26,005 | 50 | A/V | 5 |
| Corpus Christi PD | 277,454 | 400 | V | 1 |
| Houston PD | 1,953,631 | 5,300 | A/V | 12 |
| Randall County SO | 104,312 | 78 | A/V | 10 |
| **Utah** | | | | |
| Salt Lake County SO | 898,387 | 350 | A/V | 5 |
| Salt Lake City PD | 181,743 | 460 | A/V | 3 |
| Utah County SO | 368,536 | 256 | A/V | 7+ |
| **Vermont** | | | | |
| Norwich PD | 3,544 | 7 | A | |
| **Washington** | | | | |
| Marysville PD | 25,315 | 40 | A/V | 8 |
| State Patrol | 5,894,121 | 800 | A | 17 |

# Appendix C

## ILLINOIS STATUTE 18: ACCEPTABLE EXCEPTIONS TO ELECTRONIC RECORDING

Illinois Statute 18 provides that, in homicide cases, statements made as a result of custodial interrogation in a police station or *place of detention* are presumptively inadmissible if not electronically recorded. This presumption can be overcome by proof by a preponderance of the evidence that the statement was voluntary and reliable based on the totality of the circumstances. In addition, the state can use the statement after proving, by a preponderance of the evidence, any of the following exceptions:[76]

a.  The statement was made in open court, before a grand jury, or at a preliminary hearing.

b.  The statement was not recorded because it was not feasible to do so.

c.  The statement was voluntary and bears on the credibility of the defendant as a witness.

d.  The suspect requested that there be no recording, if the request is recorded.

---

[76] New York County Lawyers Association report on the electronic recording of police interrogations

e. The statement was made after routine questioning for processing.

f. The statement was made out of state.

g. The statement was made when the interrogator was unaware that a death had in fact occurred.

h. Multiple suspects were questioned, and all available recording equipment was being utilized for other suspect.

i. The statement was otherwise admissible under law.

# Appendix D

## SAMPLE INTERNAL POLICY ON ELECTRONIC RECORDING[77]
## SUBJECT: ELECTRONICALLY RECORDED INTERVIEWS

Definitions:

*Interview*:    The Broward County Sheriff's Office recognizes that communication, in the law enforcement context, is considered an art form where the detective is required to possess skills that will allow them to objectively obtain accurate and truthful information from another person. During the course of an investigation, the status of the person with whom the detective is interacting with may alternate between witness, victim, and suspect. For this reason, it is the opinion of the Broward County Sheriff's Office that the distinction between an interview and an interrogation is without significance.

*Suspect Interview:*  For our purposes, a suspect interview is defined as an interview conducted by deputies investigating an alleged crime with a person who is, when viewed objectively, based on the evidence developed to date, thought to have been involved in the crime. Witnesses and victims

---

[77] Reprinted with permission from Major Tony Fantigrassi, Broward County Sheriff's Office, FL.

are not considered suspects until or unless evidence is developed that changes their status. Electronic Recording: Electronic Recording is defined as the use of audiocassettes and/or VHS videotapes and/or DVD non-rewriteable disc, used in conjunction with VHS, DVD and/or tape recorders, to commemorate suspect interviews.

2.    Procedures:

Only suspect interviews in the crimes specified below will be electronically recorded in their entirety. All other crimes will be at the discretion of the Sheriff's Office:

Homicide

Manslaughter

Vehicular Homicide

DUI Manslaughter

Armed Robbery

Unarmed Robbery

Detonate Destructive Device W / Injury

Child Abuse

Exploitation of Elderly

Abuse of Elderly

Sexual Battery

Unlawful Sex with Minors

Kidnapping / False Imprisonment

Aggravated Battery

Extortion

Arson

3.    Whenever feasible, suspect interviews shall be conducted at the Criminal Investigations Division.

4.    Victim and witness interviews may be electronically recorded in their entirety at the discretion of the detective.

5.    Whenever feasible, suspect interviews shall be electronically recorded using VHS and/or DVD video recordings.

6.    When suspect interviews are captured on video they will be electronically captured using 3 DVD recorders and 1 VHS recorder per interview.

7.    Audiocassette recordings will be acceptable, when VHS and/or DVD video recordings are not feasible or practical.

8.    The electronically recorded suspect interview must include the giving of the suspect's Miranda rights.

9.    Any legal advice a suspect may seek during the interview process must be addressed immediately.

10.   If a suspect invokes their right to remain silent, detectives shall acknowledge their decision by informing them that they will not be able to continue speaking with them about the case.

11. Detectives may remain in the interview room with the suspect, but cannot initiate any further questioning. The suspect(s), however, do have the right to reinitiate the interview if they desire.

12. If a suspect acknowledges that it is their desire to reinitiate the interview, detectives may continue the interview, but must first clearly demonstrate, during the electronic recording, that it was solely the suspect's decision to continue without an attorney present.

13. The electronically recorded suspect interview should clearly indicate that it recounts the entire interview with the suspect.

14. Whenever feasible, there should be no relevant unrecorded dialog initiated by the interviewer prior to the electronic recording commencing.

15. Any relevant unrecorded dialog between the suspect and interviewer must be explained during any subsequent electronically recorded suspect interview. If there is no subsequent interview, the dialogue will be noted and made part of the permanent case file.

16. Explanations for any interruptions in the electronically recorded suspect interview must be given at the beginning and/or the end of the interruption, so as to minimize the speculation as to what took place during the interruption.

17.    The electronic recording will commence at the moment the suspect is placed in the Criminal Investigations interview room.

18.    The electronic recording shall not end until the time the suspect is permanently removed from the interview room, regardless of whether they are being interviewed or not.

19.    There is no expectation to privacy while the suspect is in custody. Therefore, the suspect need not be told that the interview is being recorded.

20.    Suspects will not be promised anything in return for their admissions and/or cooperation.

21.    Suspects will not be threatened or coerced into making any admissions against their free will.

22.    Detectives will not create bogus evidence and/or any deception that will "overcome the free will" of the suspect.

23.    Detectives may establish a dialogue with the suspect using language that the suspect is comfortable with and accustomed to.

24.    Derogatory or profane language may be used when part of the interview strategy.  It will be the interviewer's responsibility to articulate that strategy in any court proceedings where the use of

such language may later be questioned.

26.     When left unattended and unmonitored in the interview room, detained suspects must be restrained according to policy.

27.     Upon completion of the interview, the electronic recordings, consisting of 3 DVD discs and 1 VHS tape will be appropriately marked with the detective's initials, date and time.

28.     Two original DVD recordings will be provided to the State Attorney's Office with the intent that one original copy will be provided by the state to the defense upon discovery.   The third original DVD recording and the VHS copy will be preserved and placed into evidence.

29.     VHS copies will be furnished to the SAO upon request or in circumstances where the DVD recorders have malfunctioned.

# Appendix E

## MINNEAPOLIS POLICE DEPARTMENT'S POLICY CONCERNING ELECTRONIC RECORDING OF CUSTODIAL INTERROGATIONS AND THE USE OF MOBILE VIDEO RECORDING (MVR)[78]

**10-206 ELECTRONIC RECORDING OF CUSTODIAL INTERROGATIONS/INTERVIEWS (01/30/95) (09/13/04)**

Officers shall electronically record all custodial interrogations and interviews of suspects when the questioning occurs at a place of detention, i.e., Hennepin County Adult Detention Center (HCADC), Juvenile Detention Center (JDC), or a MPD vehicle that is equipped with Mobile Video Recording (MVR) equipment, etc. Interrogation includes any information about rights, any waiver of those rights, and all questioning. Upon completing an electronic recording of a custodial interrogation/interview, the tape(s) shall be property inventoried according to department procedures.

For further information regarding audio recordings of suspect

---

[78] The Minneapolis Police Department's Policy concerning the use of Mobile Video Recording (MVR) was reprinted from their web site: http://www.ci.minneapolis.mn.us/mpdpolicy/

interrogations/interviews in MVR-equipped vehicles, see Section 4-218 - Mobile Video Recording Equipment.

## 4-218 MOBILE VIDEO RECORDING EQUIPMENT (05/25/04)

### GENERAL OBJECTIVE

The purpose of this policy is to establish policies and procedures regarding the use of Mobile Video Recording (MVR) equipment in MPD vehicles and to establish policies and procedures regarding the storage, release, and retention of MVR videotapes.

### POLICY

- The use of MVR equipment in MPD vehicles will facilitate the collection of evidence for criminal prosecution or complaint investigation. They may also be used as a training tool for officer safety and best practices in the MPD.
- All MVR videotapes are the property of the MPD and original MVR videotapes shall remain in the sole custody of the MPD. Precinct/Unit commanders or their designees are responsible for the usage, storage, erasure, requests for copies, and recycling of videotapes intended for patrol use.
- MVR equipment shall be activated during every traffic stop and will record the traffic stop in its entirety. Officers shall inform those who ask, that video/audio recording equipment is in use. The MVR equipment is designed and installed to automatically

engage whenever emergency overhead lights are activated. Officers can also manually activate the MVR equipment.

- Officers are prohibited from altering MVR equipment in any way. Officers shall only use MVR videotapes issued by the MPD. Officers are prohibited from erasing, re-recording or tampering with MVR tapes.

- Any sworn supervisor can direct an officer to activate or deactivate MVR equipment. Officers can manually deactivate MVR equipment during non-enforcement activities, such as protecting accident scenes, traffic posts, assisting motorists, etc.

- Officers may activate MVR equipment and change the camera position at their own discretion for the following purposes:

  o To record their reasons for current or planned enforcement action;

  o To record the actions of suspects during interviews or when placed in custody;

  o To record the circumstances at crime scenes and accidents; or

  o To record any other situation as warranted.

- MVR tapes will be stored at the precinct/unit where issued. If original MVR videotape is of evidentiary value, it shall be inventoried in the Property & Evidence Unit. Property & Evidence Unit personnel are responsible for maintaining records relative to retention of MVR videotapes that are being held as evidence. MPD Stores is responsible for distributing blank MVR tapes to the precincts and units.

- An MVR-equipped vehicle can be used for off-duty employment with supervisor permission. MVR-equipped vehicles and use of MVR equipment are subject to all requirements as outlined for on-duty use.

- Unless otherwise noted, MVR videotapes shall be retained for a minimum of one year and then may be erased and/or reused. The final decision on the length of retention of non-evidentiary tapes is still under discussion with department and labor representatives and pending approval from the Minnesota Data Retention Office.

## VIDEOTAPE CONTROL & INSTALLATION

- MVR videotapes shall be sequentially numbered and clearly labeled. MVR videotapes will have a precinct/unit designation and an individually unique identifying number. Precinct/unit designations are P1, P2, P3, P4, P5, and TF (Traffic). An example of a sequential order is P1-0001, P1-0002 and P1-0003.

- Each precinct/unit shall track the installation/removal of MVR videotapes via the precinct/unit MVR Videotape Log. A printable version of this log is available on the MPD's Intranet site under "MPD Forms."

- At each precinct, shift supervisors are the only persons authorized to possess the key to the MVR trunk vault. They are also the only persons authorized to load or unload videotape into the MVR. Officers of the citywide MPD Traffic Unit are responsible for the loading/unloading and storage of videotapes used in Traffic Unit squads.

- Videotapes shall be locked within a squad's videotape vault. Once the videotape is loaded, it shall remain in the MVR vault until the overhead console display indicates the videotape has less than 30 minutes of recording time left. Officers assigned to the MVR-equipped squad shall request a supervisor to load new videotape into the MVR. Prior to loading new videotape in a squad, a supervisor shall note the following on the videotape and on the precinct videotape log:

    o Videotape number

    o Date and time tape was loaded into the MVR

    o Squad and vehicle "P" number

    o Precinct or unit

    o Supervisor's name and badge number

When videotape is removed from a squad, the supervisor shall note on the precinct/unit video log the date and time of the removal and the supervisor's name and badge number

**MVR EQUIPMENT CHECK**

Prior to each use, officers shall check to ensure that MVR equipment is operational. Before placing any MVR-equipped vehicle in service, officers shall perform the required series of checks to determine if the equipment is working properly. The MVR check will include the following:

- Position the camera pointing forward, aiming down the center of the vehicle, to accurately record the events.
- Ensure that the wireless microphone is turned on.
- Perform an audio/video test to ensure that the MVR equipment is in working order. For the audio/video test, officers shall clearly state the assigned officer name(s), badge number(s), date, squad number(s), and shift.
- In the event that the MVR monitor displays the wrong date and time, officers will verbally add the correct date and time and note the discrepancy on the motor patrol log.
- The officer's immediate supervisor shall be notified of any malfunctioning MVR equipment.

**PROPERTY INVENTORYING VIDEOTAPES**

Videotapes shall be property inventoried in the following situations:

- Any pursuit, squad accident, DWI arrest, use of force, or felony crime in which the MVR equipment was in use.
- If for any reason the officer or sworn supervisor believes the tape to be of evidentiary and/or administrative value or if the identity of someone in the video needs to be protected. In cases where evidence is recorded, it shall be noted on the videotape and in the CAPRS report.

A supervisor shall remove MVR videotapes of evidentiary value from the MVR vault and then remove the recording protection tab on the spine of the videotape. The supervisor or his/her designee, noting all changes of chain-of-custody in a CAPRS supplement, shall inventory the videotape. Officers shall note the change of chain-of-custody in a CAPRS supplement. Officers inventorying videotapes shall comply with all other Property and Evidence Unit procedures.

## REQUEST TO VIEW OR DUPLICATE VIDEOTAPES

- MPD administration shall reserve the right to view or duplicate any MVR videotape as needed.
- Evidentiary videotapes shall be viewed and/or copied under the Crime Lab's policies. The Crime Lab is responsible for documenting any changes in the chain-of-evidence and/or custody of evidentiary tapes that are being viewed or copied.
- MVR videotapes that are not being held for evidence are public information. Public requests to view or copy videotapes, or portions thereof, shall be considered in light of data practice guidelines (Minn. Stat. §13.82, Comprehensive Law Enforcement Data). Precinct/Unit commanders shall make the determination as to whether MVR videotape is released or not. All public requests to view or copy MVR videotapes must be submitted on an Office of Media Services Request Form. Officers receiving a videotape duplication request shall also

complete a MPD Data Practice Compliance Form. Printable copies of both forms are available on the MPD Intranet site under "MPD Forms."

- Both requests shall be submitted to the precinct/unit commander where the MVR videotape is assigned or stored. A precinct/unit commander or his/her designee will ensure that all requests are honored in a timely fashion. If a request cannot be honored, the commander shall provide an explanation to the requester. Prior to being released, the City Attorney may also review requests to view or copy videotapes that have criminal and/or administrative value. The Chief or his/her designee shall be advised of all media requests to view or copy videotapes.

- Once the requested portion of the MVR videotape is duplicated, the requester shall pay an appropriate duplication fee per videotape, as set by the Office of Telecommunications and Media Services. Fees shall be paid at the MPD License Unit, Room 1A, City Hall. Upon delivery of the videotape, the requester shall be given a receipt.

- Under most circumstances for public requests, the Office of Telecommunications and Media Services, Room 123, City Hall will copy MVR videotapes. For public requests, the MPD commander or their designee will provide the Office of Telecommunication and Media Services the original MVR videotape, a description of the section(s) to be copied and the number of copies requested.

- For internal requests, the MPD will provide the Office of

Telecommunications and Media Services the original videotape, copy instructions, and a blank videotape(s) for copying purposes. Upon request, copies of videotapes shall be provided to prosecutors and the courts at no charge. With the approval of precinct/unit commanders, other law enforcement agencies with a valid need will be provided a copy of MVR videotape at no charge.

• Original MVR videotapes shall be returned to the originating precinct/unit for further storage and/or reuse.

# Appendix F

## SUBJECT DATA SHEET

(Department name and address)

Name:_____Date_____Time_____

1.  In the last 24 hours, have you had any alcohol, drugs or medication? Y   N   If yes, please explain_____

    _____

2.  In the last 24 hours, how many hours of sleep have you had?

    _____

3.  How long ago did you eat your last full meal?  _____

4.  Circle the last year of school you completed:

    6  7  8      9  10  11  12      13  14  15  16      17  18  19  20

    Middle      High School          College          Post-graduate

5.  Are you presently experiencing any physical discomfort? Y  N

    If yes, explain _____

    _____

6.  Are you presently under a physician's care for any medical

    problem?  Y   N   If yes, please explain:_____

    _____

7.  In the last 12 months, have you talked to a psychologist or

    psychiatrist about an emotional or mental health problem? Y  N

    If yes, please explain: _____

    _____

8.  How would you describe your present emotional and physical

    wellbeing?

    Excellent_____

    Good _____

    Al Right_____

    Poor _____

_____          _____

Signature                          Witness

# Appendix G

# CONSENT TO ELECTRONICALLY RECORD
(Department name and address)

Interviewer:_____


I_____

hereby voluntarily consent to the electronic recording of any of my

statements or conversations while at the (<u>Department name</u>).


Date_____        Time_____


_____        _____
    Signature                    Witness


<u>FOR USE IF SUBJECT IS A MINOR</u>


I,_____, a parent (or guardian) of the above-named

interviewee, have read the forgoing and agree to its provisions.


Date_____        Time_____


_____        _____
    Signature                    Witness

# Appendix H

## STATE EAVESDROPPING LAWS[79]

**Alabama**

Ala. Code § 13A-11-30, -31: Unlawful eavesdropping is defined as the overhearing or recording of the contents of a private communication without the consent of at least one person engaged in the communication. The statute has been interpreted as creating a right to privacy in communications — specifically, a right not to have communications overheard, recorded or disclosed without consent. *Ages Group v. Raytheon Aircraft Co., 22* F. Supp. 2d 1310 (M.D. Ala. 1998).

**Alaska**

Alaska Stat. § 42.20.310: It is illegal in Alaska to use an eavesdropping device to hear or record a conversation without the consent of at least one party to that conversation, or to disclose or publish information that one knows, or should know, was illegally obtained. A person who is not a party to a private conversation who receives information from that conversation cannot legally divulge or publish the information. Alaska Stat. § 42.20.300.

**Arizona**

Ariz. Rev. Stat. Ann. § 13-3005: Interception of a wire or electronic communication by an individual who is not a party, without the consent of someone who is a party to the communication, is a felony. The electronic communications referred to in the statute include wireless and cellular calls. The overhearing of a conversation by an individual who is not present, without the consent of a party to that conversation, is also a felony. Both violations are classified as "class 5" felonies, which are the second least serious felonies in Arizona.Under the statute, consent is not required for the

---

[79] This is an abbreviated summary of the State Laws regarding consent.

taping of a non-electronic communication uttered by a person who does not have a reasonable expectation of privacy in that communication. See definition of "oral communication," Ariz. Rev. Stat. Ann. § 13-3001.A state appellate court has held that a criminal defendant's contention that police officers violated this law by recording their interviews with him without his consent was meritless because the defendant had no reasonable expectation of privacy in a police interview room. *Arizona v. Hauss*, 688 P.2d 1051 (Ariz. Ct. App. 1984).

### Arkansas
Ark. Code § 5-60-120: Intercepting or recording any wire, oral, or cellular or cordless phone conversations is a misdemeanor, unless the person recording is a party to the conversation, or one of the parties to the conversation has given prior consent. Arkansas law also criminalizes the "interception" of a message transmitted by telegraph or telephone in its "public utility" laws. Ark. Code § 23-17-107.

### California
Cal. Penal Code §§ 631, 632: It is a crime in California to intercept or eavesdrop upon any confidential communication, including a telephone call or wire communication, without the consent of all parties.  It is also a crime to disclose information obtained from such an interception. A first offense is punishable by a fine of up to $2,500 and imprisonment for no more than one year. Subsequent offenses carry a maximum fine of $10,000 and jail sentence of up to one year.  Eavesdropping upon or recording a conversation, whether by telephone (including cordless or cellular telephone) or in person, that a person would reasonably expect to be confined to the parties present, carries the same penalty as intercepting telephone or wire communications. Conversations occurring at any public gathering that one should expect to be overheard, including any legislative, judicial or executive proceeding open to the public, are not covered by the law.

### Colorado
Colo. Rev. Stat. § 18-9-303: Recording or overhearing a telephone conversation, or any electronic communication, without the consent of a party to the conversation is a felony punishable by a fine of between $1,000

and $100,000 and one year to 18 months in jail. Recording of a communication from a cordless telephone, however, is a misdemeanor. Colo. Rev. Stat. § 18-1.3-401.

**Connecticut**
Conn. Gen. Stat. § 52-570d: It is illegal to tape a telephone conversation in Connecticut without the consent of all parties. Consent should be in writing or should be given on the recording, or a verbal warning that the conversation is being taped should be included in the recording.

**Delaware**
Del. Code Ann. tit. 11, § 2402(c)(4): Delaware's wiretapping and surveillance law specifically allows an individual to "intercept" (defined as acquiring the contents of a communication through a mechanical device) any wire, oral or electronic communication to which the individual is a party, or a communication in which any one of the parties has given prior consent, so long as the communication is not intercepted with a criminal or tortious intent.
However, another Delaware privacy law makes it illegal to intercept "without the consent of all parties thereto a message by telephone, telegraph, letter or other means of communicating privately, including private conversation." Del. Code Ann. tit. 11, § 1335(a)(4). The wiretapping law is much more recent, and at least one federal court has held that, even under the privacy law, an individual can record his own conversations. *United States v. Vespe*, 389 F. Supp. 1359 (1975).

**District of Columbia**
D.C. Code Ann. § 23-542: It is legal to record or disclose the contents of a wire or oral communication where the person recording is a party to the communication, or where one of the parties has given prior consent, unless the recording is done with criminal or injurious intent. A recording made without proper consent can be punished criminally by a fine of no more than $10,000 or imprisonment for no more than five years. However, disclosure of the contents of an illegally recorded communication cannot be punished criminally if the contents of the communication have "become common knowledge or public information."

**Florida**
Fla. Stat. ch. 934.03: All parties must consent to the recording or the disclosure of the contents of any wire, oral or electronic communication in Florida. Recording or disclosing without the consent of all parties is a felony, unless the interception is a first offense committed without any illegal purpose, and not for commercial gain, or the communication is the radio portion of a cellular conversation. Such first offenses and the interception of cellular communications are misdemeanors. *State v. News-Press Pub. Co.*, 338 So. 2d 1313 (1976), *State v. Tsavaris*, 394 So. 2d 418 (1981).
Under the statute, consent is not required for the taping of a non-electronic communication uttered by a person who does not have a reasonable expectation of privacy in that communication. *See* definition of "oral communication," Fla. Stat. ch. 934.02.

**Georgia**
Ga. Code Ann. § 16-11-62: Secretly recording or overhearing a conversation held in a private place, whether carried out orally or by wire or electronic means, is criminally punishable as a felony under statutory provisions regarding invasions of privacy. However, the law expressly provides that it does not prohibit a person who is a party to a conversation from recording and does not prohibit recording if one party to the conversation has given prior consent. Ga. Code Ann. § 16-11-66.

**Hawaii**
Haw. Rev. Stat. § 803-42: Any wire, oral or electronic communication (including cellular phone calls) can lawfully be recorded by a person who is a party to the communication, or when one of the parties has consented to the recording, so long as no criminal or tortious purpose exists. Unlawful interceptions or disclosures of private communications are punishable as felonies.
The one-party consent rule does not apply, however, to the installation of a recording device in a "private place" that will amplify or broadcast conversations outside that private place. All parties who have a reasonable expectation of privacy in that place must consent to the installation of a recording device. Haw. Rev. Stat. § 803-42(b)(3).

## Idaho
Idaho Code § 18-6702: Although legislation criminalizes the interception and disclosure of wire or oral communications, it specifically allows interception when one of the parties has given prior consent. Punishment for the felony of an illegal interception or disclosure can include up to five years in prison and as much as $5,000 in fines. Anyone whose communications are unlawfully intercepted can sue for recovery of actual damages, $100 a day per day of violation or $1,000 – whichever is more. Punitive damages, litigation costs and attorney fees also can be recovered. Idaho Code § 18-6709.

## Illinois
720 Ill. Compiled Stat. Ann. 5/14-1, -2: An eavesdropping device cannot be used to record or overhear a conversation without the consent of all parties to the conversation under criminal statutes. An eavesdropping device is anything used to hear or record a conversation, whether the conversation is in person or conducted by any means other than face-to-face conversation, such as a telephone conversation.

## Indiana
Ind. Code Ann. § 35-33.5-1-5: The recording or acquiring of the contents of a telephonic or telegraphic communication by someone who is neither the sender nor the receiver is a felony and can be the basis for civil liability. Ind. Code Ann. §§ 35-33.5-5-4, -5.

## Iowa
Iowa Code § 727.8: It is a misdemeanor in Iowa under general criminal laws to tap into a communication of any kind, including telephone conversations, unless the person listening or recording is a sender or recipient of the communication, or is openly present and participating in the conversation. Thus, one party to a communication generally may record it without the consent of the other parties.

## Kansas
Kan. Stat. Ann. § 21-4001: Unlawful eavesdropping consists of secretly listening to, recording, or amplifying private conversations or using any

device to intercept a telephone or wire communication "without the consent of the person in possession or control of the facilities for such wire communication." Violations are misdemeanors. A criminal breach of privacy, punishable as a misdemeanor as well, occurs when any means of private communication is intercepted without the consent of the sender or receiver. Divulging the existence or contents of any type of private communication, whether carried out by telephone or even letter, is also a misdemeanor if the person knows the message was intercepted illegally. Kan. Stat. Ann. § 21-4002. The state's highest court has interpreted the eavesdropping and privacy statutes to sanction one-party consent for taping of conversations and in interpreting both statutes stated: "In other words, any party to a private conversation may waive the right to privacy and the non-consenting party has no Fourth Amendment or statutory right to challenge the waiver." *Kansas v. Roudybush*, 686 P.2d 100 (Kan. 1984).

### Kentucky

Ky. Rev. Stat. Ann. § 526.010: It is a felony to overhear or record, through use of an electronic or mechanical device, a wire or oral communication without the consent of at least one party to that communication. Ky. Rev. Stat. Ann. § 526.020.

Anyone who inadvertently hears a conversation transmitted through a wireless telephone on a radio receiver does not violate the eavesdropping statute, but if that same conversation is recorded or passed on to others without the consent of a party to the original conversation, a violation occurs. Ky. Att'y. Gen. Op. 84-310 (1984).

### Louisiana

La. Rev. Stat. § 15:1303: Unless a criminal or tortious purpose exists, a person can record any conversations transmitted by wire, oral or electronic means to which he is a party, or when one participating party has consented. A violation of the law, whether by recording or disclosing the contents of a communication without proper consent, carries a fine of not more than $10,000 and jail time of not less than two and not more than 10 years at hard labor.

## Maine

Me. Rev. Stat. Ann. tit. 15, § 709: Interception of wire and oral communications is a "Class C" crime under the state criminal code, and an interceptor is someone other than the sender or receiver of a communication who is not in the range of "normal unaided hearing" and has not been given the authority to hear or record the communication by a sender or receiver.

## Maryland

Md. Code Ann., Courts and Judicial Proceedings § 10-402: It is a felony to intercept a wire, oral or electronic communication unless all parties to the communication have consented. But all-party consent will not make the recording legal if there is a criminal or tortious purpose behind it.Massachusetts

Mass. Ann. Laws ch. 272 , § 99: It is a crime to record any conversation, whether oral or wire, without the consent of all parties in Massachusetts. The penalty for violating the law is a fine of up to $10,000 and a jail sentence of up to five years.

## Michigan

Mich. Comp. Laws § 750.539c: A private conversation legally cannot be overheard or recorded without the consent of all participants. Illegal eavesdropping can be punished as a felony carrying a jail term of up to two years and a fine of up to $2,000.

## Minnesota

Minn. Stat. § 626A.02: It is legal for a person to record a wire, oral or electronic communication if that person is a party to the communication, or if one of the parties has consented to the recording – so long as no criminal or tortious intent accompanies the recording. Unlawful recordings, or disclosure of their contents if there is knowledge or reason to know of the illegal acquisition, carry maximum penalties of imprisonment for five years and fines of $20,000. In addition, civil liability for violations statutorily can include three times the amount of actual damages or statutory damages of up to $10,000, as well as punitive damages, litigation costs and attorney fees. Minn. Stat. § 626A.13.

A federal court has interpreted the statute to allow a parent or guardian to consent to taping on behalf of a minor child. *Wagner v. Wagner*, 64 F. Supp.2d 895 (D. Minn. 1999).

## Mississippi

Miss. Code Ann. §§ 41-29-501 to -537: It is generally a violation of Mississippi law to intercept and acquire the contents of wire, oral or other communications with a mechanical or electronic device. The law against interception of communications applies neither to a "subscriber" to a telephone who "intercepts a communication on a telephone to which he subscribes," nor to members of the subscriber's household. Miss. Code Ann. § 41-29-535, *Wright v. Stanley*, 700 So.2d 274 (Miss. 1997) (state law prohibition on wiretapping did not apply to former wife who intercepted communications on her own telephone).

## Missouri

Mo. Rev. Stat. § 542.402: Only an individual who is a party to a wire communication, or who has the consent of one of the parties to the communication, can lawfully record it or disclose its contents unless it is intercepted for the purpose of committing a criminal or tortious act. Recording or disclosing the contents of a wire communication by all other persons is a felony.

## Montana

Mont. Code Ann. § 45-8-213: It is a violation of privacy in communications under state law to record a conversation with a hidden electronic or mechanical device without the knowledge of all parties to the conversation, but the law does not apply to public officials or employees speaking in the course of their duties, to anyone speaking at a public meeting, or to anyone who has been warned of the recording.

## Nebraska

Neb. Rev. Stat. § 86-290: A person who is a party to a wire, electronic or oral communication, or who has obtained prior consent from a party, can record or disclose the contents of that communication without violating the law, so long as there is no criminal or tortious purpose behind the recording or disclosure. Illegal interceptions are felonies that can be punished with fines up to $10,000 and five years in prison. Neb. Rev. Stat. § 28-105.

In addition, anyone whose conversation has been illegally intercepted is specifically authorized to recover through a civil action monetary damages, litigation costs and attorney fees. Neb. Rev. Stat. § 86-297.

## Nevada

Nev. Rev. Stat. Ann. § 200.620: The Nevada wiretapping statute provides that it is a crime for anyone to "intercept" or disclose the contents of any wire communication, but that no illegal activity occurs when the interception is made "with the prior consent of one of the parties to the communication" and "an emergency situation exists."

In December 1998, the state's highest court stated in a 3-2 decision that the wiretapping statutes require that an individual obtain the consent of all parties before taping a telephone conversation, and thus, that an individual who tapes his own telephone calls without the consent of all participants unlawfully "intercepts" those calls. *Lane v. Allstate Ins. Co.*, 969 P.2d 938 (Nev. 1998).

In addition, it is a criminal invasion of privacy to secretly listen to, record or disclose the contents of any private conversation "engaged in by other persons" through use of any mechanical or electronic device, "unless authorized to do so by one of the persons engaging in the conversation." Nev. Rev. Stat. Ann. § 200.650.

## New Hampshire

N. H. Rev. Stat. Ann. § 570-A:2: It is a felony to intercept, or disclose the contents of, any telecommunication or oral communication without the consent of all parties. However, it is a misdemeanor for a party to a communication, or anyone who has the consent of only one of the parties, to intercept a telecommunication or oral communication.

## New Jersey

N.J. Stat. § 2A:156A-3: Interception of any wire, electronic or oral communication, or disclosure of the contents of such communication by someone having reason to know of the interception, is a crime. The disclosure of intercepted information is not a crime, however, if the contents of the communication have "become public knowledge or public information."

In addition, an interception is legal if the interceptor is a party to the communication, or one of the parties has given prior consent, so long as no criminal or tortious intent is present. Nonetheless, even if a person is a subscriber to a particular telephone, that person cannot consent to the recording of conversations on that telephone to which he is not a party. N.J. Stat. § 2A:156A-4.

### New Mexico

N.M. Stat. Ann. § 30-12-1: A criminal interference with communications occurs when anyone intercepts, records or discloses the contents of any message sent by telephone or telegraph without the consent of a sender or receiver. Illegal interceptions are misdemeanors. Illegal interceptions carry the potential for civil liability for the greater of actual damages, $100 per day of violation or $1,000, along with punitive damages, attorney fees and litigation costs. N.M. Stat. Ann. § 30-12-11.

An intermediate appellate court has stated that in New Mexico, "one who voluntarily enters into a conversation with another takes the risk that the other person on the line may memorize, record or even transmit the conversation." *New Mexico v. Arnold*, 610 P.2d 1214 (N.M Ct. App. 1979), *rev'd on other grounds*, 610 P.2d 1210 (N.M. 1980).

### New York

N.Y. Penal Law §§ 250.00, 250.05: It is a Class E felony to overhear or record a telephonic or telegraphic communication if one is not the sender or receiver, or does not have the consent of either the sender or receiver. It also is a crime for someone not present to overhear or record any conversation or discussion without the consent of at least one party to that conversation.

### North Carolina

N.C. Gen. Stat. § 15A-287: It is a Class H felony to intercept or disclose the contents of a wire, oral or electronic communication without the consent of at least one party to the communication, The statute defines wire communications to exclude the radio portion of a cordless telephone call that is transmitted between a cordless telephone handset and base unit. N.C. Gen. Stat. § 15A-287.

In addition, communications transmitted in a manner accessible to the general public, radio transmissions of aircrafts, ships or vehicles, and law enforcement radio communications, can be legally intercepted.

## North Dakota

N.D. Cent. Code § 12.1-15-02: Anyone who is a party to a communication, or who has obtained prior consent from someone who is a party to the communication, may legally record or disclose the contents of any wire or oral communication as long as they do not have criminal or tortious intent. Recording or disclosing the contents of a communication without one party's consent or with criminal or tortious intent is a felony carrying a maximum penalty of a $5,000 fine and imprisonment for five years. N.D. Cent. Code § 12.1-32-01.

## Ohio

Ohio Rev. Code Ann. § 2933.52: Intercepting, recording or disclosing the contents of a wire, oral or electronic communication if a person is a participant, or has obtained the consent of at least one participant, is legal unless it is accompanied by a criminal or tortious intent.

Under the statute, consent is not required for the taping of a non-electronic communication uttered by a person who does not have a reasonable expectation of privacy in that communication. See definition of "oral communication," Ohio Rev. Code Ann. § 2933.51. The Ohio Supreme Court has held that prisoners do not have a reasonable expectation of privacy in their communications, for purposes of the wiretapping law. *State v. Robb*, 723 N.E.2d 1019 (Ohio 2000).

## Oklahoma

Okla. Stat. tit. 13, § 176.4: Anyone who is a party to a wire, oral or electronic communication or who has obtained consent from a party can lawfully record or disclose the contents of that communication, so long as he does not do so in furtherance of a criminal act.

Under the statute, consent is not required for the taping of a non-electronic communication uttered by a person who does not have a reasonable expectation of privacy in that communication. *See* definition of "oral communication," Okla Stat. tit. 13, § 176.2.

## Oregon

Or. Rev. Stat. §§ 165.535, 165.540: It is illegal to obtain or divulge a telecommunication or radio communication, unless one is a party or has obtained consent from at least one party to the conversation. It is illegal to obtain or divulge an oral communication unless all parties to the communication are informed that their conversation is being obtained. Certain enumerated exceptions apply. Violations are punishable by a maximum sentence of $5000 or one year in jail.

Or. Rev. Stat. § 165.543: It is also a misdemeanor to intercept a wire or oral communication where one is not a party to the communication, and none of the parties to the communication have consented.

Under the statute, consent is not required for the taping of a non-electronic communication uttered by a person who does not have a reasonable expectation of privacy in that communication. *See* definition of "oral communication," Or. Rev. Stat. § 133.721.

## Pennsylvania

18 Pa. Cons. Stat. §§ 5703, 5704: It is a felony to intercept any wire, oral or electronic communication without the consent of all participants. It also is a felony to disclose or use the contents of a communication when there is reason to know those contents were obtained through an illegal interception.

Under the statute, consent is not required for the taping of a non-electronic communication uttered by a person who does not have a reasonable expectation of privacy in that communication. *See* definition of "oral communication," 18 Pa. Cons. Stat. § 5702.

A trial court has held that a communication protected by the legislation is one in which there is an expectation that it will not be recorded by any electronic device, rather than one in which there is a general expectation of privacy. Thus, the fact that a participant may believe he will have to reveal the contents of a communication, or that other parties may repeat the contents, does not necessarily mean that he would have expected that it would be recorded, and it is the expectation that the communication would not be recorded that triggers the wiretapping law's protections. *Pennsylvania v. McIvor*, 670 A.2d 697 (Pa. Super. Ct. 1996), *petition for appeal denied*, 692 A.2d 564 (Pa. 1997).

## Rhode Island

R.I. Gen. Laws § 11-35-21: State law expressly allows the recording and disclosure of the contents of any wire, oral or electronic communication by a party to the communication or with the prior consent of one of the parties, so long as no criminal or tortious purpose exists.

Under the statute, consent is not required for the taping of a non-electronic communication uttered by a person who does not have a reasonable expectation of privacy in that communication. *See* definition of "oral communication," R.I. Gen. Laws § 12-5.1-1.

## South Carolina

S.C. Code Ann. §§ 17-30-20, 17-30-30: It is a felony to intercept, disclose or use a wire, electronic or oral communication, unless it is done with the consent of at least one party to the communication.

Under the statute, consent is not required for the taping of a non-electronic communication uttered by a person who does not have a reasonable expectation of privacy in that communication. *See* definition of "oral communication," S.C. Code Ann. § 17-30-15.

## South Dakota

S.D. Codified Laws § 23A-35A-20: It is a felony to intercept or record any wire or oral communication unless the person recording is a sender or receiver of the wire communication or has obtained the consent of either the sender or receiver, or unless the person recording is present during the oral communication or has obtained the consent of one party to the oral communication.

Under the statute, consent is not required for the taping of a non-electronic communication uttered by a person who does not have a reasonable expectation of privacy in that communication. *See* definition of "oral communication," S.D. Codified Laws § 23A-35A-1.

Generally, the consent of one participant in any communication to the recording removes it from the type of interception prohibited under the South Dakota wiretapping statute. *South Dakota v. Braddock*, 452 N.W.2d 785 (S.D. 1990); *Midwest Motor Sports, Inc. v. Arctic Cat Sales, Inc.*, 144 F. Supp.2d 1147 (D. S.D. 2001).

**Tennessee**

Tenn. Code Ann. § 39-13-601: A person who is a party to a wire, oral or electronic communication, or who has obtained the consent of at least one party, can lawfully record a communication and divulge the contents of the recorded communication unless he has a criminal or tortious purpose for doing so. Violations are punishable as felonies with jail sentences of between two and 12 years and fines not exceeding $5,000. Tenn. Code Ann. §§ 39-13-602, 40-35-111.

Under the statute, consent is not required for the taping of a non-electronic communication uttered by a person who does not have a reasonable expectation of privacy in that communication. *See* definition of "oral communication," Tenn. Code Ann. § 40-6-303.

**Texas**

Texas Penal Code § 16.02: So long as a wire, oral or electronic communication – including the radio portion of any cordless telephone call – is not recorded for a criminal or tortious purpose, anyone who is a party to the communication, or who has the consent of a party, can lawfully record the communication and disclose its contents.

Under the statute, consent is not required for the taping of a non-electronic communication uttered by a person who does not have a reasonable expectation of privacy in that communication. *See* definition of "oral communication," Texas Code Crim. Pro. Art. 18.20.

**Utah**

Utah Code Ann. § 77-23a-4: An individual legally can record or disclose the contents of any wire, oral or electronic communication to which he is a party, or when at least one participant has consented to the recording, unless the person has a criminal or tortious purpose in making the recording.

Under the statute, consent is not required for the taping of a non-electronic communication uttered by a person who does not have a reasonable expectation of privacy in that communication. *See* definition of "oral communication," Utah Code Ann. § 77-23a-3.

## Vermont

There is no legislation specifically addressing interception of communications in Vermont, but the state's highest court has held that surreptitious electronic monitoring of communications in a person's home is an unlawful invasion of privacy. *Vermont v. Geraw*, 795 A.2d 1219 (Vt. 2002); *Vermont v. Blow*, 602 A.2d 552 (Vt. 1991).

The state's highest court, however, also has refused to find the overhearing of a conversation in a parking lot unlawful because that conversation was "subject to the eyes and ears of passersby." *Vermont v. Brooks*, 601 A.2d 963 (Vt. 1991).

## Virginia

Va. Code Ann. § 19.2-62: Despite the fact that it is generally a felony to intercept or disclose the contents of any wire, oral or electronic communication under state law, the recording or disclosing of communications by a party, or with the consent of a party, is specifically permitted.

Under the statute, consent is not required for the taping of a non-electronic communication uttered by a person who does not have a reasonable expectation of privacy in that communication. *See* definition of "oral communication," Va. Code Ann. § 19.2-61; *Belmer v. Commonwealth*, 553 S.E.2d 123 (Va. App. 2001).

## Washington

Wash. Rev. Code § 9.73.030: All parties generally must consent to the interception or recording of any private communication, whether conducted by telephone, telegraph, radio or face-to-face, to comply with state law. The all-party consent requirement can be satisfied if "one party has announced to all other parties engaged in the communication or conversation, in any reasonably effective manner, that such communication or conversation is about to be recorded or transmitted." In addition, if the conversation is to be recorded, the requisite announcement must be recorded as well.

Whether a communication is considered "private" under the statute depends on the factual circumstances. Among the factors considered are the subjective intent of the parties; the reasonableness of their expectation of privacy; the duration and subject matter of the communication; the location of the communication and the presence of third parties; and the relationship between the consenting party and the non-consenting party. *State v. Townsend*, 57 P.2d 255 (Wash. 2002). A person who sends e-mail to another person has consented to the "recording" of that e-mail. *Id.*

## West Virginia
W. Va. Code § 62-1D-3: Recording a wire, oral or electronic communication, or disclosing its contents, is not a violation of West Virginia law when the person recording is a party to the communication or has obtained consent from one of the parties, as long as the recording is not accompanied by a criminal or tortious intent.

## Wisconsin
Wis. Stat. § 968.31: A person who is a party to a wire, electronic or oral communication, or who has obtained prior consent from one party, can legally record and divulge the contents of the communication, unless he does so for the purpose of committing a criminal or tortious act.

Under the statute, consent is not required for the taping of a non-electronic communication uttered by a person who does not have a reasonable expectation of privacy in that communication. *See* definition of "oral communication," Wis. Stat. § 968.27.

## Wyoming
Wyo. Stat. § 7-3-702: It is legal for a party to a wire, oral or electronic communication to record that communication, and it is legal for anyone to record with the consent of one of the parties to a communication, unless the communication is intercepted to further a criminal or tortious purpose.

Under the statute, consent is not required for the taping of a non-electronic communication uttered by a person who does not have a reasonable expectation of privacy in that communication. *See* definition of "oral communication," Wyo. Stat. § 7-3-701.

# Legal Decisions

# Index

# About the Authors

**David M. Buckley** graduated from the University of Illinois with a Bachelor of Arts degree in Sociology, and went on to earn a Masters of Science degree from Reid College. He has been employed by John E. Reid & Associates since 1981 and was named the Director of their Denver office in 1983. In 1990 he developed a seminar for child protection workers designed to improve their investigative skills and is the Director of that program. Mr. Buckley is a licensed detection of deception examiner and has personally conducted over 8,000 interviews and interrogations. He has been teaching interviewing and interrogation seminars for 23 years throughout the United States and several International locations. Mr. Buckley has written a variety of specialized training manuscripts, and has produced a number of training videotapes, audiotapes and CD-ROMs in the specialized area of interviewing and interrogation.

**Brian C. Jayne** is a licensed detection of deception examiner and has been employed by John E. Reid and Associates since 1978. He has a Bachelor of Arts degree in Criminal Justice and a Master's degree in the Detection of Deception. Mr. Jayne has published dozens of articles in the area of interviewing and interrogation, including studies investigating the validity and reliability of the polygraph technique and behavior symptom analysis. He has taught interviewing and interrogation techniques to thousands of investigators during seminars conducted across the United States and Canada. Mr. Jayne has written chapters in a number of legal text books and is the co-author of three books addressing the fields of interviewing and interrogation. He has consulted as an expert witness in criminal and civil cases and offered testimony in state, Federal and Military trials.